PERCEPTION TOME I

Preface

Not going to waste too much time on me. I am Paul Noumessi, and I am a Simple Observer. I grew up in Cameroon, raised by parents who were both loving and deeply disciplined. They instilled in me the value of structure, respect, and persistence. In our home, nothing was taken lightly. Every action had a purpose, every moment a lesson. My early years were rooted in a straightforward, no-nonsense approach to life, yet behind it was an undeniable warmth—a sense of love that formed the bedrock of my existence.

As I grew older, life began to broaden. I moved to the United States, an entirely new world that opened my eyes to different ways of thinking, being, and living. Here, I encountered perspectives I had never considered, questions I had never asked myself. I began to understand that the way we see the world is shaped by our backgrounds, our environments, and our experiences. And the more I traveled, the more I encountered cultures that expanded and redefined my sense of reality. From the streets of Europe to the vibrant landscapes of South America, and the diverse warmth of Canada, I immersed myself in different worlds. These experiences fueled a deep, burning curiosity in me—a need to understand the threads that connect us all, beyond borders, beyond cultures, beyond the familiar.

It was through this journey of learning and questioning everything that I began to form an idea. This idea, which had been simmering beneath the surface for years, started to crystallize. It grew from a whisper into something undeniable—a realization that everything we experience is filtered through the lens of perception. And that simple yet profound understanding became the foundation for this book.

Perception isn't just a collection of ideas—it's an exploration. It's an invitation for you to question, to dig deeper, and to expand your awareness of what's possible. Through these chapters, you'll be guided to examine not just the world outside, but the world within. Every belief, every thought, every assumption you've ever held can be questioned, and in that questioning lies the freedom to experience life anew.

A Glimpse into the Journey

In the first chapter, we dive into **The Nature of Perception**, exploring how our minds shape the reality we see. You'll discover that perception is not a passive process, but an active creation. This chapter will set the foundation for understanding how deeply our worldview influences everything we think, feel, and experience.

From there, we move to **Breaking the Boundaries of the Self**, where I share insights into how we limit ourselves without realizing it. Here, you'll learn how our perceptions of ourselves define what we believe we can achieve—and more importantly, how to break free from these limitations.

Perception of Time and Reality will push the boundaries even further, asking you to rethink your relationship with time. Is time truly linear, or is there more to our experience of it? You'll engage with concepts that challenge the very core of what you believe to be true about existence.

In **Cultural Perceptions and Global Perspectives**, I draw upon my experiences from living and traveling around the world. This chapter explores how our upbringing and surroundings shape our worldview and how stepping into new cultures can shift our understanding of ourselves and others.

Finally, in **The Shift: Conscious Living and Creating Your Reality**, I'll guide you toward using perception as a tool for transformation. This chapter is about taking everything you've learned and applying it, so you can begin consciously creating the life you want to live.

Through each chapter, I aim to ignite your curiosity and inspire you to think beyond the ordinary, beyond the surface. This book is meant to be a guide—one that opens doors to new ways of thinking, being, and experiencing the world around you.

Introduction: The Lens of Perception

- **What is perception?**

  - How our beliefs, conditioning, and senses shape our experience of the 3D world.

  - The invitation to look beyond surface appearances and challenge inherited perceptions.

- **The purpose of this journey**

  - Realigning with our true nature, dissolving limiting beliefs, and expanding consciousness.

  - Awakening to the interconnectedness of all life, both seen and unseen.

Chapter 1: Time — The Illusion and the Infinite

- **Linear vs. non-linear time**

  - How the perception of time controls our experience.

  - The eternal "Now" and living beyond the limitations of past and future.

- **The timeless self**

  - Understanding our eternal nature in relation to time.

Chapter 2: Death — The End or a Transition?

- **What is death, truly?**

  - Perception of death as a finality vs. as a transformation or shift in consciousness.

  - Personal growth through understanding death as part of life's eternal flow.

- **Continuing beyond the physical**

  - Connection with life beyond the body— higher dimensions, consciousness beyond form.

Chapter 3: The Purpose of Life — Remembering Who We Are

- **Why are we here?**

  - Exploring the purpose of life and the meaning behind human existence.

- o The idea of **destiny**—a guiding force that helps us fulfill our potential and grow through experience.

- **Living with purpose**

  - o Aligning our daily lives with our highest potential and greater purpose.

Chapter 4: Dimensions — Beyond the Physical

- **What are dimensions?**

  - o Expanding awareness beyond 3D reality into higher planes of existence.

  - o How different dimensions coexist and influence one another.

- **Accessing multidimensional awareness**

  - o Practical tools for expanding perception to connect with the higher realms.

Chapter 5: Empowerment — Reclaiming Your Infinite Power

- **Understanding the self as infinite**

  - o Realizing the true self beyond the ego, as a limitless being.

o Breaking free from fear and disempowerment.

- **Co-creating with the universe**

o The power of intention, thought, and energy in shaping your reality.

Chapter 6: God — Redefining Divinity

- **What is God?**

o Moving beyond traditional definitions to perceive God as the infinite source of love, energy, and creation.

o The nature of oneness—God within all things, including us.

- **Living as a reflection of divinity**

o Embracing the divine within yourself and others to live in harmony with all existence.

Chapter 7: Prayer and Manifestation — Conversations with the Infinite

- **The true nature of prayer**

- o Prayer as an intimate connection with the universe, not just asking but aligning.

  - o Embodying prayer as a state of being, not just a moment of supplication.

- **The art of manifestation**

  - o How to consciously create your reality by aligning thought, feeling, and vibration with the infinite.

  - o The role of surrender and trust in the process of manifestation.

Chapter 8: Cosmic Forms of Life — We Are Not Alone

- **Expanding our awareness to other life forms**

  - o The existence of beings from higher dimensions, other planets, and parallel realities.

  - o What these cosmic relationships mean for humanity's evolution and shared consciousness.

- **How to connect and coexist**

- o Developing our intuitive senses to communicate and co-create with beings of light, energy, and wisdom from other realms.

Chapter 9: Living Fully Connected — Merging Spirit with the Physical

- **What does it mean to live fully connected?**

  - o Living as a whole, balanced being, integrating the spiritual and the material.

  - o The importance of grounding spiritual awareness in everyday life.

- **Embodying the infinite in a 3D world**

  - o Practical ways to live in alignment with higher truths while engaging in physical reality—relationships, work, creativity, and service.

Conclusion: The Infinite Journey

- **Life as an ongoing expansion of consciousness**

  - o Acknowledging the ever-unfolding nature of existence.

- o Encouraging the reader to continue exploring their own perception, knowing they are part of the vast, interconnected web of All That Is.

Breakdown Of Perception Series

This book is divided into three parts: **Tome 1**, **Tome 2**, and **Tome 3**. Each section explores a different layer of perception, moving from the individual to the collective, and finally into the cosmic understanding of reality. Together, they form a comprehensive breakdown of how we, as humans, perceive the world around us, and how those perceptions shape our lives, cultures, and the universe itself.

We often go through life as if we are looking through a foggy window—what we see is shaped by beliefs, fears, and inherited ideas that blur the truth of who we are and what life really is. This book is an opportunity to wipe that window clean, to help you see clearly, beyond the veils that have clouded your perception for so long. If you accept this invitation, what you hold in your hands is not just a book, but an instruction manual—a guide to transforming how you perceive existence itself.

The way you perceive life *is* your life. When you change your perception, everything changes. This first volume in the *Perception* series will serve as a personal compass, showing you how to realign your inner world—your thoughts, your beliefs, your understanding of time, death, purpose, and empowerment—so that your outer experience of life becomes more expansive, peaceful, and fulfilling. It is designed to gently guide you out of old patterns of seeing and into a more profound and liberating view of existence.

A Journey of Three Stages

This book is the first of a trilogy, each part designed to take you deeper into the mystery and truth of life. You are beginning with *Perception: Tome 1*, which is focused on the perception of **Existence** at an individual level. Who are you, really? What is the nature of time, death, and purpose? How can you tap into your infinite nature and live fully connected to the deeper truth of life? This first volume is about you—your personal journey of awakening to your true self.

But this is only the beginning. In the second volume, we will explore *Perception* at a **societal** level. How do we collectively shape the world we live in? What are the stories we've agreed upon as a society, and how do they affect how we perceive ourselves and each other? This second tome will examine the shared lenses that cultures, traditions, and systems use to filter reality. It will be a deep dive into how we can shift society's perception toward a more harmonious, connected, and awakened collective experience.

Finally, in the third volume, we will expand even further, exploring *Perception* on a **cosmic** level. How does our individual and societal perception fit into the grand, universal scheme of things? What is our connection to the cosmos, to other forms of life, to dimensions beyond the physical? The third tome will explore perception beyond the boundaries of Earth and humanity, into the infinite, cosmic web of existence.

These three books form a cohesive journey. Starting with the self, expanding to society, and ultimately opening to the universe. Each tome invites you to peel back the layers of perception, to question the world as you've known it, and to awaken to a broader, more interconnected reality.

The Power of Perception

To understand how profoundly perception shapes our life, let's start with something simple: Have you ever noticed how two people can experience the same event but have completely different reactions? One person may feel joy, while the other feels frustration. The event is the same, but the perceptions are not. It's not the world that changes—it's how we see it. And how we see it determines how we experience it.

In a way, perception is like wearing tinted glasses. If your glasses are foggy or dark, the world seems dim, confusing, and heavy. But if your lenses are clear, if they allow light and clarity through, the same world appears vibrant, full of possibilities, and alive with meaning. Most of us are wearing some version of foggy glasses. We've been conditioned to see life through limiting beliefs, through a narrow understanding of time, fear of death, and a distorted sense of purpose. This book is about removing those lenses—about cleaning the glasses so you can see life in its true, luminous form.

Take the idea of time, for example. We're often taught to believe that time is a linear force, marching forward, dragging us along with it. We worry about running out of time, fear aging, and regret the past. But what if time isn't a straight line at all? What if it's more like a vast ocean, where all moments—past, present, and future— are always flowing together, accessible at any moment? When you begin to shift your perception of time, your relationship to life fundamentally changes. You stop fearing the future or clinging to the past, and you start living fully in the present—where life is truly happening.

This book is full of ideas like that—ideas that challenge the way you've been taught to see the world, not to create confusion but to offer a more expansive, liberating perspective. Each chapter is designed to be a stepping stone, gently guiding you from where you are now to a deeper, more empowered understanding of reality.

An Invitation to Question Everything

To engage with this journey, you must be willing to question everything. Be curious. Be open. This isn't about adopting new beliefs or dogmas. It's about opening your mind to the possibility that there's more to life than you've been told. It's about remembering the parts of yourself that have been hidden beneath layers of conditioning and fear.

Imagine this: Your perception of life is like a painting you've been staring at for years. You think you know every detail—the colors, the shapes, the figures. But then one day, you step back and realize that there's a whole new part of the painting you hadn't noticed before. The figures start to shift, the colors become more vibrant, and suddenly, you're seeing the whole picture, not just the piece you had been focusing on. This is what shifting perception feels like. It's not about replacing the old painting; it's about expanding your view to see the bigger, more beautiful picture that's always been there.

Through this book, you are being invited to expand the boundaries of what you think is possible. To look at your life with new eyes and recognize the infinite potential that lies in every moment. You are being called to step into the fullness of who you truly are—a being of infinite potential, deeply connected to all that is.

A Loving Reminder

Remember, this journey is not about perfection or "getting it right." There is no test here. This is a process of awakening, of deepening your relationship with life, with yourself, and with the universe. Be gentle with yourself as you move through these ideas. Some may resonate immediately, while others may take time to settle. That's okay. Transformation is a process, and each person's path is unique.

Know that as you read these pages, you are supported. You are not alone in this journey. You are part of a larger wave of awakening, a collective shift in consciousness that is happening across the world right now. The fact that you are holding this book is a sign that you are ready to take the next step, to expand your perception, and to live more fully connected to the truth of who you are.

Where We Begin

As we dive into this first tome, focused on the perception of **individual existence**, I invite you to pause and reflect: What if everything you've known about time, death, purpose, and reality was just one perspective? What if there is a more expansive way to see it all—one that brings you peace, joy, and connection to something far greater than yourself?

This is your opportunity to open to that possibility. To awaken to your infinite nature. To see life in a new way and, as a result, to live it differently.

Introduction: What is Perception?

Perception is the lens through which you experience life. It shapes every interaction, colors every emotion, and determines what you believe to be possible. But here's the thing: most of us never question this lens. We assume the way we see the world is the way the world truly is. We rarely ask ourselves: *What if my perception is incomplete? What if I've been conditioned to see only part of the picture?*

At its core, perception is not just about your senses—what you see, hear, touch, taste, or smell. It's about how your mind interprets the world based on your beliefs, upbringing, culture, and experiences. These elements combine to create a filter through which every moment of your life is understood. This filter isn't inherently bad, but it is limited. It is shaped by forces outside of you—your family's ideas, society's expectations, and historical narratives you've inherited without ever really examining.

Imagine perception as a pair of glasses you've worn since birth. The lenses of these glasses are made up of all the beliefs, habits, and judgments you've absorbed from the world around you. Over time, these lenses get fogged up with assumptions and past experiences. The world outside hasn't changed, but your ability to see it clearly has. **The invitation of this book is to clean those lenses, to see life through fresh eyes, and to challenge the assumptions that have shaped your reality.**

How Our Beliefs and Conditioning Shape Our Experience

Much of what we take as "truth" is actually a reflection of our conditioning. For example, think about your beliefs around success. Most of us are taught that success means achieving certain things—financial security, a stable career, recognition from others. But have you ever stopped to ask where that belief came from? Did you choose it, or was it handed to you by your environment?

Consider how powerful conditioning can be. In the 1960s, a psychologist named Albert Bandura conducted an experiment that demonstrated how children learned aggression simply by watching adults. The famous **Bobo doll experiment** showed that children imitated what they saw, often without even thinking. We do the same in adulthood, mimicking the beliefs and behaviors we see around us, rarely questioning why we follow certain paths or hold certain ideas.

Our beliefs, often unconsciously adopted, act like invisible scripts running in the background of our lives. They tell us what's possible, what's worth striving for, and what we should fear. But these beliefs are not absolute—they are simply learned perceptions. If you were raised in a different country or culture, your belief systems might be entirely different, and you'd see the world in a whole new light.

Here's a simple truth: **your perception of reality is shaped by what you've been taught to believe about yourself and the world.** And just as easily as it was formed, it can be reshaped. The journey of this book is about becoming aware of these underlying beliefs and choosing consciously whether they serve you or limit you.

The Invitation to Look Beyond Surface Appearances

Let's take a step further. Imagine an iceberg floating in the ocean. What you see above the surface—the visible tip—is only a fraction of its true size. The majority of the iceberg lies beneath the water, unseen and untouched by the waves. **Your perception of life is like that iceberg.**

The visible world—the events, the situations, the people around you—are just the surface. Beneath that surface lies a vast, deeper reality that you have the potential to explore.

We've been trained to focus on surface appearances. A person's behavior, the way they dress, or their job title becomes a shorthand for understanding who they are. But much like the iceberg, what you see on the surface rarely tells the full story. The same goes for situations in your life. What appears to be a challenge might be an opportunity in disguise. What looks like failure could be setting you up for a breakthrough.

This book invites you to look beneath the surface—to question what you've always assumed to be true, and to explore the deeper layers of reality that are often hidden from sight. When you begin to question your surface perceptions, life opens up in ways you may never have imagined. A challenge transforms into a stepping stone. A fear becomes an invitation to grow. And you, yourself, are revealed to be far more powerful than you've ever believed.

Realigning with Our True Nature

So, what's the purpose of this journey? Why shift your perception at all?

At the heart of this work is the process of **realigning with your true nature**. Your true nature is the infinite, timeless essence that exists beyond the roles you play, the beliefs you've been given, or the fears you've inherited. It's the part of you that is connected to everything—beyond the limitations of this three-dimensional world, beyond the boundaries of time and space. It's the **"you"** that existed before you learned who you were supposed to be, and the "you" that will continue long after this lifetime.

Imagine a river that flows freely and naturally. That's how we are meant to live—aligned with our true essence, moving with the current of life. But over time, our beliefs, fears, and conditioning build dams in that river, blocking the flow. We get stuck, caught in patterns that no longer serve us, living in a limited reality. By shifting your perception, by dissolving the beliefs that no longer serve you, you allow that river to flow again. You reconnect with your authentic self and experience life in its full, expansive potential.

Dissolving Limiting Beliefs and Expanding Consciousness

Let's talk about **limiting beliefs**. These are the beliefs that create walls around your perception, making you feel like life is a narrow hallway with few doors. "I'm not good enough." "I don't have enough time." "Life is hard." These are common scripts that run beneath the surface, shaping your reality. They are like invisible chains that hold you back, often without you realizing it.

But the good news is this: **beliefs are not facts.** They are thoughts you've repeated so often that they became your truth. And if you can adopt them, you can also release them. One of the key purposes of this journey is to help you dissolve these limiting beliefs so that you can expand your consciousness, moving beyond the small self that is trapped in doubt, fear, or judgment.

Think of it this way: If you lived your whole life inside a room with no windows, you might believe that the room is all there is. But what if, one day, you discovered a door? You open it, step outside, and find yourself standing in a vast, open field. Suddenly, you realize that the room was never your true reality—it was just the container you had been living in. **Your beliefs are like**

that room. Once you challenge them, once you open the door, you step into the expansiveness of life itself. There are no walls, only infinite possibilities.

Awakening to the Interconnectedness of All Life

When you begin to expand your consciousness, something extraordinary happens. You start to awaken to the **interconnectedness of all life**. You realize that you are not a separate, isolated being moving through a random world. You are part of a vast, intricate web of existence that connects every living thing.

Think of the world like a forest. Each tree stands individually, rooted in its own space, with its own branches and leaves. But beneath the surface, the roots of all the trees are interconnected, forming a network that allows them to communicate, share resources, and support each other. **Life is like that forest.** On the surface, we appear separate—each living our own individual lives—but at a deeper level, we are all connected. Our thoughts, our actions, our perceptions ripple out into the world, affecting everything around us.

This realization is both humbling and empowering. It means that the way you perceive life doesn't just shape your individual experience—it ripples out to affect the whole. And as you expand your perception, as you align with your true nature, you begin to contribute to the awakening of the collective consciousness.

This journey is about more than just understanding life differently. It's about living **from** that deeper understanding, awakening to the truth that you are not separate from life, but an integral part of its unfolding. As you move through the pages of this book, you will be invited to question the perceptions that no longer serve you, to realign with your true self, and to expand your awareness to include the vast, interconnected reality that exists both within and beyond you.

You are here for a reason. Welcome to the journey of *Perception.*

Chapter 1: Time — The Illusion and the Infinite

Linear vs. Non-linear Time

The concept of **linear time**—that life moves forward in a straight, unchanging line—is one of the most ingrained beliefs we carry. It's reinforced by everything around us: the ticking of the clock, the progression of age, the history books that tell us what happened before and what will happen next. Linear time tells us that the past is behind us, the present is now, and the future is something we must move toward, step by step.

But here's a hard truth: *linear time is a construct*. It's a useful construct, yes—it helps us organize our days and plan for the future. But it is not an absolute truth. It is simply one way of perceiving reality, and it limits our experience in profound ways.

Imagine a train track that stretches straight into the horizon. When you're on the train, you see the landscape moving by, station after station, in sequential order. It feels like time is moving forward, like you're progressing from one place to the next. But if you could step off the train and look at the entire track from above, you'd see that all the stations exist simultaneously. From this higher perspective, the beginning, middle, and end of the journey all coexist in the same space. They are all "there," but it's your movement through them that creates the illusion of time flowing.

This is the concept of **non-linear time**. Imagine time as a sphere, where all moments exist at once—interconnected, influencing one another. This is not just an abstract idea. Science, too, hints at the fluidity of time. Albert Einstein's theory of relativity suggests that time is not a constant; it bends and warps depending on where we are and how fast we're moving. What this means is that time is **relative**—it behaves differently based on your perspective.

Think about your own life. There have been moments where time seemed to slow down, right? Perhaps during a joyful experience, like falling in love or creating something meaningful, where hours seemed to vanish in an instant. Then there are moments where time feels painfully slow, like during grief or boredom, when minutes seem to stretch on endlessly. This should tell you something important: time is flexible. It moves and bends according to our perception.

If you can grasp this, you begin to see that you're not trapped on a train moving toward some future destination. You are, in fact, standing in that infinite field of possibility. Your experience of time is fluid, and you have more agency over it than you've been led to believe.

The Eternal "Now"

So, if time isn't linear, what is it? The answer lies in something both incredibly simple and endlessly profound: the **eternal Now**.

The **Now** is the only thing that truly exists. The past is a memory—something your mind replays like a video stored in your brain. The future is an expectation—something you imagine but have yet to experience. Neither the past nor the future exists in reality. They exist only in your mind. The **present moment** is the only place where life happens, the only place where you truly exist. Everything else is either a projection of the mind (the future) or a recollection of a previous experience (the past).

But let's go deeper. The present moment, the Now, is not just a fleeting second between what has already happened and what will come next. The **Now** is *eternal*.

It is always here. Every moment you have ever experienced has happened in the Now. Every moment you will experience will happen in the Now. The future is nothing more than the Now you haven't reached yet, and the past is the Now that has already been.

To fully grasp the **eternal Now**, think about the way we experience music. Music doesn't exist as isolated notes—it exists in the flow of sound, in the seamless movement from one note to the next. But where does the music *actually* happen? It's not in the past note, and it's not in the future note. The music is only ever happening in the Now—in the moment of sound, as it vibrates and fills the space. Time works the same way. Your life isn't a series of past events strung together by future possibilities; it's a continuous, eternal unfolding happening in the present moment.

When you live fully in the **Now**, you begin to realize that you are not bound by time in the way you once thought. You are not running out of time, you are not losing time, and you are not waiting for the future to deliver something better. Life is happening right now. And when you anchor yourself in that understanding, you stop feeling like life is passing you by, and start realizing that life is something you're actively experiencing in each moment.

Living Beyond the Past and Future

One of the great challenges we face is how much of our time is spent living either in the past or the future. We dwell on past mistakes, past heartbreaks, past experiences, and we let those memories shape who we are today. At the same time, we constantly project ourselves into the future—planning, worrying, hoping. But here's the catch: *neither the past nor the future exists right now.*

Let me give you an analogy. Imagine your mind as a library filled with books. The past is a book you've already read, sitting on a shelf. The future is a book you haven't picked up yet. Now, you can choose to sit and endlessly re-read that past book, pouring over its pages, obsessing about what you could have done differently. Or you can spend all your time reading the introduction to the future book, trying to figure out what it will be about before it's even written. But in both cases, you're missing the book that's actually open in front of you— the book of the Now, which is the only one you can truly engage with.

When you live in the past, you are bound by it. You carry the weight of old stories, of regrets, of things you can't change. When you live in the future, you are always striving, always waiting for something better, something different, something "more" than what is right here in front of you. But living in the Now releases you from both of those prisons. It frees you from the weight of past mistakes and the pressure of future expectations. **The Now is where your power lies.**

This doesn't mean ignoring the lessons of the past or neglecting to plan for the future. It means understanding that your real life—the only life you will ever experience—is unfolding *right now*. The past is only relevant insofar as it informs this moment. The future is only important insofar as it is shaped by the choices you make in the Now.

The Timeless Self

Now let's bring this closer to you. If time is not linear, and if the only reality is the present moment, what does that say about **you**? Who are you, really?

The truth is, you are a **timeless being**. The part of you that observes life—the awareness that is reading these words right now—has no age, no expiration date, no boundaries. Think about it: you have lived through countless moments, countless experiences, and yet, the "you" that experiences them—the witness—remains unchanged. Sure, your body may change, your circumstances may change, but the deep essence of who you are is timeless. It is the same essence that has existed through every phase of your life and will continue to exist beyond this one.

Imagine your life like a film reel. Each moment is a frame on that reel, and you are the light passing through it, projecting the movie onto the screen of your consciousness. The frames may change—the scenes of your life shift from one experience to the next—but the light, the awareness that makes the movie visible, remains constant. **That light is your timeless self.** It is the part of you that exists beyond the passing of time, beyond the ticking of clocks. It is the eternal observer of your experience.

The Timeless Self: Understanding Our Eternal Nature in Relation to Time

Now, let's explore a profound concept: **the timeless self**. This is the part of you that exists beyond the constraints of time. You are not just a body moving through life, aging with every passing year. At your core, you are consciousness—an eternal, infinite presence that experiences time but is not bound by it.

Think of it this way: Imagine you are the sky. The clouds, the sun, the storms—they all pass through the sky, changing its appearance. But the sky itself remains unchanged. It holds all these experiences, but it is not altered by them. **Your consciousness is like the sky**, vast and untouched by the passing of time. The events of your life are like the clouds and weather—they come and go, but the essence of who you are remains the same, eternal and unchanging.

When you identify with your timeless self, you begin to see that you are more than your thoughts, more than your memories, and more than your plans. **You are the awareness behind all of it.** Time passes, but you remain. The body may age, but the essence of who you are is timeless, beyond the reach of minutes, hours, or years.

This understanding shifts everything. When you realize that you are not bound by time, the fear of aging, the pressure to achieve, and the anxiety of "running out of time" start to dissolve. You begin to live from a place of deep presence, where you are no longer controlled by external clocks or internal deadlines. **You are free to simply be.**

Conclusion: Stepping Into Timelessness

As you move through this chapter, I invite you to take a step back from the way you've always perceived time. Start noticing how much of your energy is spent in the past or future, and gently guide yourself back to the present. Practice living in the **Now**, where life is unfolding, moment by moment, in its full richness.

This is not just about changing your ideas; it's about shifting your experience. **The more you center yourself in the eternal Now, the more expansive and liberated your life will become.** You will begin to move beyond the illusion of linear time and tap into the timeless essence of who you truly are.

Time may be an illusion, but your presence—here and now—is very real. And it is through that presence that you can unlock the infinite potential of your life.

Chapter 2: Death — The End or a Transition?

Let's talk about death. Not just as an idea, but as a reality. For many, the thought of death sends a chill down the spine, tightening the chest with fear, a reflexive recoil from something we are taught to avoid, to not think about too deeply. But why? Why is death this looming specter that we're so afraid to face? **What is death, truly?**

Is death the final curtain, the absolute end of all that we are? Or could it be a doorway—a transition into something else, something beyond the body, beyond the mind, beyond what we know?

We're taught to fear death because it feels like an unknown. And as humans, we've been conditioned to believe that the unknown is dangerous. But pause for a second. Is the unknown inherently bad? Think about every significant transformation in your life. Each change, each step forward into a new chapter—wasn't there some fear in that unknown? And yet, here you are, continuing, growing. Maybe the fear wasn't telling you about the danger, but simply reflecting the fact that you were on the edge of something new.

Death, then, is not the enemy. It's an inevitable part of the flow of life. So instead of avoiding the conversation, let's dive into it.

What is Death, Really?

Let's start with a question that most people avoid: *What do you actually believe about death?* Forget what society says, forget what religion tells you—what do *you* believe? Do you believe death is the end, that consciousness simply fades into oblivion? Or do you have a quiet sense, maybe buried deep, that death is more of a shift—a passageway from one state of being to another?

Most of us have been conditioned to think of death as a **finality**. We fear it because it feels like we're losing everything—our bodies, our relationships, our achievements, our very identity. And in a world that celebrates accumulation—whether it's wealth, status, or experiences—death seems like the ultimate thief, stripping away everything we've worked to build.

But let's challenge that. **Is death really an end?** Look at nature. Nothing ever truly ends. The seasons cycle. The day turns into night, and night becomes day. The trees shed their leaves, but they don't die—they prepare for new growth. Even stars, which seem eternal, eventually collapse into themselves, only to become the birthplace of something new—a nebula, a new star, a black hole. **Everything transforms.**

You are part of that same cycle. You, too, are part of nature's flow. Your body may decay, but does that mean your essence—your consciousness—ceases to exist? If energy cannot be destroyed, only transformed, why would your consciousness be any different?

Think about a candle. When it burns out, where does the flame go? It doesn't "die." The energy, the heat, and the light dissipate, but the flame was never something static or permanent—it was an interaction of elements. When those elements change, the form changes, but the energy continues to exist in another way. **Death, too, is a change in form, not the destruction of life.**

Perception of Death as Transformation

To grasp this more deeply, consider how we view the body. We're trained to see ourselves as the body, and so we think, "When the body dies, I die." But let me ask you something: *Are you your body?*

When you close your eyes and listen to your thoughts, when you feel your emotions, when you imagine, dream, or reflect—where are you experiencing these things? Certainly not just in the physical form. The body is a vehicle, a container. But **you**—the awareness that feels, thinks, and is aware of its own existence—exist beyond that container.

Think about technology: your phone, your computer. The hardware—the body—is necessary to interact with the software, but the software itself can exist beyond the physical device. You can take that software and transfer it, update it, expand it, and it still functions, even if the hardware changes. In the same way, **your consciousness—your true essence—isn't tied to the body**. It uses the body as an interface to experience the world, but it is not limited to it.

This shifts our understanding of death from **finality** to **transformation**. When the body dies, it is not the end of who you are. It's the end of one form of experience, yes, but not the end of your essence. This is a truth that shows up in every major spiritual tradition. But you don't need religion or doctrine to feel it. You've already felt it in moments of deep silence, of stillness, when you sense that there's something far greater than the temporary, material world around you.

Personal Growth Through Embracing Death

Here's another truth that's hard to hear but essential to embrace: **Death is happening all the time.**

We think of death as something that only happens at the end of life, but in reality, it's present in every moment. Every breath is the death of the previous one. Every decision is the death of another potential path. Every day, parts of you—cells, thoughts, ideas—are dying to make way for the new.

Embracing death as a natural, constant process allows you to grow. It teaches you to let go of what no longer serves you. Every fear, every attachment, every limiting belief must die for something new to take its place. This is why, in many ancient traditions, death is associated with rebirth. The phoenix doesn't just rise from the ashes by accident. It must first burn, let go of its old form, to experience its own renewal.

When you face death—not just physical death, but the small deaths of ego, fear, and identity—you grow. Every version of yourself that dies gives birth to a more expansive version. That's what life is: a constant flow of death and rebirth. Each ending makes room for a new beginning, a new possibility. This is why confronting death directly, with open eyes, leads to personal liberation. When you stop fearing death, you stop fearing life.

Continuing Beyond the Physical

Let's get into the mechanics now: What happens beyond the physical?

When the body dies, when the heart stops beating, and the breath fades, where does consciousness go? This is the great mystery. But if we understand that consciousness is not tied to the body, we can begin to explore the possibility that it continues beyond it. **You don't disappear.**

Let's consider this: Have you ever had a dream so vivid that you woke up wondering if it was real? In that dream, your body was at rest, but you were very much alive—feeling, thinking, experiencing. What if death is like stepping into that dream state, but without waking up? What if death is the ultimate expansion of consciousness, beyond the limitations of the physical?

When people describe near-death experiences, they often talk about seeing their body from above, observing it from a distance. They speak of moving through tunnels of light, encountering an overwhelming sense of peace, of connection, of love. Whether or not you believe these stories is beside the point. What they illustrate is this: **Consciousness is capable of existing beyond the body.**

This isn't just a comforting idea; it's reflected in quantum physics. The idea that reality is not just physical matter but fields of energy, interconnected, with consciousness potentially being a fundamental part of the universe. We are not separate from the fabric of existence; we are woven into it. When the body ceases to function, consciousness doesn't end—it simply moves, expands, shifts into another state.

Imagine a wave in the ocean. When it reaches the shore, it seems to "end," but in truth, the water that made up that wave simply returns to the ocean, to continue in another form. **You are like that wave.** Your physical form is temporary, but the consciousness that animates it is eternal, flowing through and beyond the body, returning to the vast ocean of existence.

Connection with Life Beyond the Body

So, what does this mean for us? It means that death isn't the final goodbye we've been taught to fear. It's a return, a re-connection with something greater. Those we've lost haven't vanished; they've transitioned. Their consciousness, their essence, continues beyond what our physical senses can perceive.

Imagine a radio broadcasting a signal. You can't see the signal, but you know it's there. When the radio breaks, the signal doesn't disappear—it's just not being picked up in the same way. **The same goes for us.** When the body dies, the signal of our consciousness doesn't stop; it just moves beyond the physical plane.

This understanding should change how we live. If death is not the end, if our essence continues beyond the body, then why do we live as if time is running out, as if every moment is a race against the clock? When we embrace the truth that life continues, we stop fearing its end, and in doing so, we can live more fully, more freely, more openly.

Embracing the Unknown with Curiosity

Death is still an unknown. But as we've seen, the unknown isn't inherently bad. It's a space of endless possibility, of transformation, of expansion. And when we stop seeing death as a threat, we stop seeing life as something to defend. Instead, we can embrace life as something to explore, to experience fully, knowing that the flow of existence is continuous, always leading us forward.

So ask yourself: What would change in your life if you stopped fearing death? How would you live differently if you knew that death is not an end, but simply a continuation?

Let that truth sink in. **You are more than your body, more than this moment, and certainly more than the fear of death.**

Chapter 3: The Purpose of Life — Remembering Who We Are

There is a question that echoes in the back of nearly every mind, at least at some point in life: *Why am I here? What is the purpose of all of this?*

It's a question that haunts some, inspires others, and yet remains elusive for many. Society offers many ready-made answers: you're here to succeed, to contribute, to be productive, to leave a legacy. But does that truly answer the deeper longing within? Is that really why we came into this world—to follow a script written by others?

This chapter invites you to go deeper, beyond the surface, beyond societal definitions of success, to explore the **true purpose of life**: the reason *you* are here, now, in this moment. We're not looking for a generalized "one-size-fits-all" answer. We are searching for something far more profound—something that connects to the very core of your being, something that awakens the truth you may have forgotten.

This is about remembering who you really are.

Why Are We Here?

Let's start with a question that's been asked for millennia: *Why are we here?* Why, out of infinite possibilities, do we exist in these bodies, in this moment, in this specific life? What is the purpose of human existence?

From a young age, we are often taught that life has a linear path. You're born, you grow, you achieve, you contribute, and then, eventually, you leave. We're encouraged to believe that purpose is something we "achieve" by external standards—whether it's through career success, wealth, recognition, or by following some socially accepted path. But I'm going to challenge that belief, right here and now.

Purpose is not something you achieve. It's something you remember.

You didn't come into this world empty, waiting to be filled with meaning. You came in *with* meaning, with purpose already woven into the very fabric of your being. Purpose is not a goal in the distance that you need to chase; it's something that emerges naturally when you align with who you truly are.

Think of a tree. It doesn't spend its time questioning whether it's fulfilling its purpose. The seed contains all the potential for the tree to grow, to reach toward the sky, to provide shelter and bear fruit. The tree's purpose is inherent in its nature, and it fulfills that purpose simply by **being what it was meant to be**. It doesn't need to achieve anything beyond that, nor does it need external validation to confirm its value. It just grows and expresses its essence, step by step, moment by moment.

You are no different from that tree.

The core of your purpose is already within you. The challenge, then, is not to "find" your purpose but to remember it—to clear away the layers of conditioning, fear, and doubt that obscure your connection to that deeper truth.

The Idea of Destiny: A Guiding Force

Now, let's introduce the concept of **destiny**. For some, destiny feels like a heavy word, as if it means that life is predestined, with no freedom to make choices. But what if we approached destiny not as a rigid path, but as a **guiding force**—a direction, a calling, an inner compass that leads you toward growth, expansion, and fulfillment?

Think of destiny as a river. The river has a direction, a flow, but within that flow, there are countless ways to move. You can float easily with the current, swim against it, or drift toward different shores. The river doesn't force you in one direction, but its natural flow will guide you toward the ocean—the greater whole. **Destiny is like that river**, gently guiding you toward your higher potential, but always allowing you the freedom to choose how you navigate it.

You have free will. You have the power to choose your actions, your path, your responses to life's challenges. But underlying those choices is this sense of **destiny**—a potential waiting to be fulfilled, a higher calling that invites you to grow, to evolve, to become the fullest version of yourself.

Here's the truth: **Your destiny is not about what you accomplish externally, but about who you become internally**. The real purpose of life is to remember your true nature—to awaken to the infinite potential that exists within you and express that through every moment of your life. Destiny is not an external prize to be won; it's an internal journey of becoming.

Living With Purpose: Aligning With Your True Self

Once you begin to grasp that your purpose is already within you, the question becomes: *How do I live with purpose? How do I align my life with this deeper truth?*

Living with purpose doesn't mean you have to quit your job, abandon your responsibilities, or embark on some grand quest. Purpose isn't about the *what*; it's about the *how*. **How** are you showing up to each moment? Are you living in alignment with your inner truth, or are you constantly trying to meet external expectations?

When you live with purpose, you begin to **align** your actions, your choices, and your daily life with your highest potential. You start paying attention to what feels expansive, what lights you up, what makes you feel connected to something greater than yourself. Living with purpose is not about chasing some external goal or arriving at a final destination. It's about bringing your authentic self into every moment, every decision, every interaction.

Your Highest Potential: A Life of Expansion

Let's dive deeper. **Your highest potential** isn't about reaching some peak where everything is perfect and complete. It's about constantly expanding, constantly growing, and constantly evolving. Just like a tree doesn't stop growing after it reaches a certain height, neither do you.

Living with purpose means recognizing that **your life is a continuous unfolding**, and each moment is an opportunity for growth. Your highest potential is not static; it's dynamic, constantly shifting as you evolve. When you align with your true nature, you begin to recognize the opportunities for growth in every situation—whether it's a challenge, a relationship, or even a mundane task.

Let's bring this down to a more practical level. Think about the daily routines in your life. You wake up, go to work, interact with people, return home. On the surface, it might seem like just another ordinary day. But what if you approached each of those moments with a sense of **purposeful awareness**?

When you're aligned with your purpose, even the smallest actions become infused with meaning. The way you speak to someone, the choices you make, the energy you bring to a situation—each of these moments is an opportunity to express your deeper truth, to embody your authentic self. Purpose is not about the *task* itself; it's about the **intention** behind the task. When you act with intention, when you're aligned with your true nature, every action, no matter how small, becomes an expression of your highest potential.

The Illusion of External Achievement

Here's a hard truth: **External achievements will never fulfill your inner purpose**. Society places immense pressure on us to measure our worth through what we accomplish—career success, financial stability, recognition from others. And while there's nothing wrong with external success, it is not a substitute for the deeper sense of fulfillment that comes from living in alignment with your true purpose.

Think of external achievement as a **mirage**. It looks like it will quench your thirst, like it will satisfy your need for meaning, but once you reach it, it disappears, leaving you searching for the next goal, the next milestone. Many people spend their lives chasing after this mirage, believing that once they achieve X—whether it's a promotion, a house, or a certain level of recognition— they will finally feel complete. But completion, wholeness, and purpose come from within, not from external validation.

Living with purpose means understanding that while external success can be a byproduct of alignment, it is not the goal. The goal is to be true to yourself, to express your inner potential, and to live in a way that feels authentic to you. Everything else—whether it's success, recognition, or achievement—will naturally follow, but it won't define you.

Destiny as Expansion: A Journey of Becoming

One of the greatest misunderstandings about purpose and destiny is that they are fixed, unchangeable, and final. But this couldn't be further from the truth. **Your purpose is always evolving**, just as you are. It's a dynamic process of becoming, not a static endpoint.

Imagine destiny not as a finish line you're racing toward, but as a wide, open landscape, filled with possibilities. **Destiny is about expansion**—about continuously stepping into a larger, more expansive version of yourself. Your purpose unfolds with each step you take. Every choice, every action, every experience is an opportunity to grow, to expand, and to evolve into the person you were meant to be.

Think of your life like a painting. With every decision you make, every experience you embrace, you're adding another brushstroke to that canvas. The masterpiece is never finished—it's always evolving, always expanding, always becoming more. **You are both the artist and the painting**, simultaneously creating and being created by the choices you make and the purpose you embody.

Awakening to Your True Purpose

So, how do you awaken to your true purpose? How do you begin to live in alignment with who you really are?

It starts with **listening**—listening to the quiet voice within that knows what feels true to you. Purpose doesn't shout; it whispers. It's the subtle pull you feel toward something that excites you, challenges you, or calls you to grow. It's the sense of fulfillment that arises when you're doing something that feels deeply aligned with your authentic self.

To awaken to your purpose, you must be willing to question the beliefs you've inherited about what life *should* be. You must be willing to let go of the need for external validation and look within to discover what lights you up. **Purpose is not something you find outside of yourself; it's something you uncover within**.

This process of awakening to your purpose is not always easy. It requires courage, vulnerability, and a willingness to step outside of the comfort zones society has built for you. But the rewards are immense. When you live in alignment with your true purpose, life becomes more vibrant, more meaningful, and more expansive. You become a conscious participant in the unfolding of your own destiny, and every moment becomes an opportunity to express your highest potential.

Conclusion: Purpose as a Way of Being

Ultimately, **your purpose is not something you achieve; it's something you embody**. It's not a destination but a way of being, a way of living that is aligned with your true nature. It's about becoming who you already are—removing the layers of conditioning and fear that have covered up your inner truth.

As you move forward in life, remember that your purpose is always evolving, always expanding, and always available to you. You don't have to chase it, and you don't have to earn it. You only have to remember it and live from that place of deep alignment, trusting that you are exactly where you need to be.

You are here for a reason. And that reason is to grow, to evolve, and to express the infinite potential that exists within you.

Chapter 4: Dimensions — Beyond the Physical

Most of us live in a three-dimensional world. We wake up, eat, work, sleep, repeat—all within the confines of what we can see, touch, hear, and measure. This physical reality feels concrete and reliable, and we believe it defines the totality of existence. But what if this is just one layer of a much larger, more complex reality? What if the physical world is only the surface of a deeper, multidimensional experience?

This chapter is an invitation to look beyond the limits of physical perception and expand your understanding of existence into **higher dimensions**. We're going to break down what dimensions are, how they coexist, and most importantly, how you can begin to tap into this expanded awareness. You don't have to be a scientist or a mystic to explore these concepts; you just have to be open to the possibility that life is much bigger than what you've been taught to see.

What Are Dimensions?

To understand dimensions, we first need to challenge how we perceive reality. Imagine living in a two-dimensional world—like a drawing on a piece of paper. If you lived there, you could only move forward, backward, left, or right. The concept of "up" or "down" wouldn't exist for you. Now imagine trying to explain to someone living in that world what it's like to live in a three-dimensional world, where you can also move up and down. They'd have a hard time understanding it because it's beyond their perception.

That's similar to how we experience **higher dimensions**. We live in the three-dimensional world, where everything has length, width, and height. We perceive time as a fourth dimension, moving forward in a linear way. But just as a two-dimensional being wouldn't be able to comprehend the third dimension, we find it difficult to imagine higher dimensions beyond the fourth.

So what are these higher dimensions? In essence, they are planes of existence that extend beyond the physical and temporal dimensions we experience daily. They are layers of reality that exist alongside our own, but they are not always perceivable with our physical senses. Think of them as different frequencies on a radio dial. Just because you're tuned into one station doesn't mean the others aren't broadcasting. The signals are still there, even if you're not hearing them.

Higher dimensions represent expanded levels of consciousness, energy, and experience. They are not separate from our world—they coexist with it. And just like you can move up and down in the third dimension, in higher dimensions, you can move through levels of consciousness, understanding, and awareness that transcend physical limitations.

Expanding Awareness Beyond the 3D World

So how do we begin to access these higher dimensions? How do we tap into realities that aren't immediately obvious to us? The key lies in expanding our **awareness**—opening our minds to perceive beyond the five physical senses.

Think of this: You experience the world through your senses, but those senses are limited by design. You see only a tiny fraction of the light spectrum, you hear only a narrow range of sound frequencies, and your touch is limited to physical contact. This doesn't mean that what you can't see, hear, or feel doesn't exist—it just means it's beyond your current perception.

This is where the concept of **multidimensional awareness** comes in. When you expand your awareness, you begin to sense beyond the physical. You start to pick up on subtle energies, intuitive insights, and higher frequencies that are constantly around you but go unnoticed by most.

To access these higher dimensions, you don't need special equipment or advanced training—you just need to become more present, more attuned to what is already there. This can happen in small, almost imperceptible ways at first. Maybe you start noticing how you feel a certain energetic "vibe" in certain spaces or around certain people. Maybe your dreams become more vivid, or your intuition sharper. These are signs that your awareness is expanding beyond the physical world.

Think of it like tuning a radio. When you first start turning the dial, you may hear static. But as you get closer to the frequency you want, the signal becomes clearer, and soon, you can hear the full broadcast. Your mind works the same way. As you open yourself to the possibility of higher dimensions, your awareness becomes the "dial" through which you begin to perceive realities that were previously hidden from view.

How Different Dimensions Coexist

Now, let's get into the mechanics of how **different dimensions coexist.** It's important to understand that higher dimensions are not "out there" somewhere. They are *here*, right now, existing alongside this physical reality. The problem is, most of us are only tuned into the frequency of the third dimension, and so that's all we experience.

Imagine this: You're sitting in a room with multiple layers of sound. On one level, there's the hum of the air conditioner. On another, the sound of birds chirping outside. And beyond that, faint voices in the distance. These sounds don't cancel each other out—they coexist, but your mind tunes in and out based on where you place your attention. Dimensions work similarly. The third dimension is the most obvious to us because it's the one we are most conditioned to perceive. But higher dimensions are also present, waiting for us to attune to them.

In these higher dimensions, time doesn't function the way it does in the third dimension. In the third dimension, we experience time as linear, a progression from past to present to future. But in higher dimensions, time becomes **non-linear**. All moments exist simultaneously, much like the frames of a film reel. What we perceive as the past, present, and future are all happening *now*, but we experience them sequentially in the third dimension.

In higher dimensions, the concept of separation begins to dissolve. In the third dimension, we see ourselves as separate beings, distinct from others, from nature, and from the universe. But in higher dimensions, the interconnectedness of all things becomes apparent. You begin to experience reality as a unified field of consciousness, where every action, thought, and energy is part of a greater whole. **Oneness**—the idea that everything and everyone is interconnected—is not just a philosophical concept in these dimensions; it's a lived reality.

Accessing Multidimensional Awareness

So how do you begin to access this **multidimensional awareness**? It starts with **presence**. The more you are fully present in the current moment, the more you begin to tune into these subtle dimensions of existence.

Meditation is one of the most powerful tools for expanding your awareness. When you quiet the mind, you remove the noise of daily distractions, allowing yourself to attune to higher frequencies. In this stillness,

you can begin to sense energies, insights, and dimensions
that exist beyond the physical.

Another way to access multidimensional awareness is
through **intuition**. Intuition is the inner knowing that
bypasses logic or reasoning. It's the feeling you get when
something "just feels right" or the quiet nudge that tells
you to avoid a certain situation. This inner knowing is
your connection to higher dimensions. The more you
trust your intuition, the more you strengthen your ability
to navigate multidimensional reality.

Let's be clear: accessing higher dimensions doesn't
mean leaving the physical world behind or becoming
disconnected from reality. It's about **expanding** your
experience of reality, embracing the fact that the physical
world is just one layer of a much larger, richer existence.
You can exist fully in the third dimension while also
being aware of and connected to higher dimensions. In
fact, the more attuned you become to higher dimensions,
the more enriched and meaningful your physical life
becomes.

Practical Ways to Expand Your Awareness

1. **Meditation and Mindfulness**: Spend time daily
    in silence, focusing on your breath and allowing

your thoughts to settle. In this stillness, pay attention to subtle shifts in your awareness. This is where you begin to tune into higher dimensions.

2. **Pay Attention to Your Energy**: Notice how you feel in certain places or around certain people. Do you feel energized, drained, or neutral? This is your sensitivity to the energies that exist beyond the physical.

3. **Trust Your Intuition**: When you get a strong gut feeling about something, trust it. This is your connection to the higher dimensions speaking to you. The more you follow your intuition, the clearer these signals will become.

4. **Engage in Nature**: Nature is a powerful bridge to higher dimensions. Spend time in natural settings and allow yourself to feel the interconnectedness of life. Notice how being in nature shifts your awareness and opens you up to deeper levels of understanding.

5. **Dream Work**: Pay attention to your dreams. Often, in the dream state, we are more attuned to higher dimensions. Keep a journal by your bed

and record your dreams when you wake up. Over time, you may begin to notice patterns, messages, or insights that come through.

Living in Both Worlds: The Integration of Dimensions

As you expand your awareness and begin to perceive these higher dimensions, it's important to stay grounded in the physical world. **Living in both worlds**—the physical and the multidimensional—doesn't mean rejecting one for the other. It means embracing both as part of a greater, unified existence.

You may start to notice that the more attuned you become to higher dimensions, the more fluid and interconnected your life in the physical world becomes. You might find yourself moving through life with greater ease, clarity, and purpose, no longer feeling constrained by the limitations of the third dimension. Challenges and obstacles begin to feel less daunting because you're no longer seeing them from a limited, third-dimensional perspective. Instead, you're seeing them in the context of a much larger, more expansive reality.

Life in the third dimension becomes richer, more meaningful, and more connected when you begin to

integrate higher dimensions into your awareness. You are not just a physical being—you are a multidimensional being, capable of experiencing life on multiple levels of reality. The more you align with this truth, the more fully you will embody the infinite potential that exists within and around you.

Conclusion: Embracing the Multidimensional Reality

This chapter is an invitation to break free from the limitations of three-dimensional thinking and begin embracing the **multidimensional reality** of existence. You are not bound by the physical world, nor are you limited to the narrow perception of life that most of us have been taught. You are a multidimensional being, living in a universe that is rich, complex, and deeply interconnected.

The more you open yourself to this expanded awareness, the more you will experience life in its fullness. You will move beyond the surface of things, beyond the limitations of time and space, and into a reality where everything is possible, everything is connected, and you are a vital part of the grand, infinite whole.

Chapter 5: Empowerment — Reclaiming Your Infinite Power

The word "empowerment" is thrown around a lot in today's world. It's in motivational speeches, self-help books, and on countless social media posts. But what does it really mean to be empowered? Is empowerment simply about having more control over your life? Or is it something deeper, something that goes beyond external success, beyond confidence, beyond personal achievements?

In this chapter, we're going to strip away the superficial understanding of empowerment and dive into the heart of what it truly means to reclaim your **infinite power**. We'll explore how empowerment is not about gaining control over the outside world, but about remembering who you are at your core—a limitless being with the power to shape reality from within.

This isn't just about "feeling" empowered; it's about stepping into the **authentic, expansive power** that is your birthright.

Understanding the Self as Infinite

The first step to reclaiming your infinite power is understanding who you really are. And I'm not talking about who you are in terms of your roles, achievements, or personality traits. I'm talking about the **self that exists beyond the ego**, beyond the mind, beyond the body.

You are not just a collection of your experiences, your thoughts, or even your emotions. Those are layers—important, yes, but not the essence of who you are. Think of them as the waves on the surface of the ocean. The waves are real, but they're temporary and ever-changing. Beneath those waves is the vast, deep ocean itself—the **infinite self**, which remains steady, untouched by the shifting tides above.

The problem is, most of us have been conditioned to believe that we are the waves. We identify with our thoughts, our limitations, our struggles, and our successes, thinking they define us. But this is a limited way of seeing ourselves. The **truth** is that you are the ocean itself. You are infinite consciousness, capable of expanding far beyond the confines of the mind, the ego, or the body.

To truly **empower yourself**, you must recognize that your power doesn't come from the outside world—it comes from this deep, eternal, infinite part of you.

Breaking Free from Fear and Disempowerment

We live in a world that often teaches us to be afraid. Afraid of failure, afraid of rejection, afraid of loss, and perhaps most subtly but most dangerously, afraid of our own power. We're taught to play small, to fit in, to follow the rules. And in doing so, we end up giving away our power without even realizing it.

But here's the thing: **No one can truly take your power from you**—only you can give it away. And we give it away by believing in our limitations. Every time we think, "I'm not good enough," "I don't deserve this," or "I'm not capable," we chip away at our own potential. These are the mental shackles that keep us in a state of disempowerment.

Let's break this down further. Imagine your mind as a vast, open sky. Clouds of fear, doubt, and insecurity pass through it, but they are not the sky itself. The sky remains vast, expansive, and untouched. You are the sky—not the clouds. Your fears and doubts are temporary; they pass through, but they do not define you.

Most people live as if they are the clouds, identifying with every passing fear or limiting belief. But true empowerment comes when you realize that these clouds—these fears—are simply **illusions**, and they have no real power unless you give it to them.

To break free from disempowerment, you must stop identifying with the clouds and remember your true nature as the vast, open sky. When you do, the clouds lose their power. The fears and doubts may still arise, but they no longer control you. You are free.

Reclaiming Your Infinite Power

So, how do you begin to reclaim your infinite power? First, you must understand that **power is not about control**. It's not about forcing outcomes or manipulating circumstances to fit your desires. True power is rooted in **alignment**—alignment with your true self, with the universe, and with the flow of life. You don't need to "grab" power from the outside world because you already have it within you. **Empowerment is about remembering that you are the source of your own power.** It's about realizing that the power to shape your reality doesn't come from controlling external factors— it comes from aligning with the truth of who you are.

Here's an analogy: Think of yourself as a lighthouse. The light inside the lighthouse represents your infinite power—your connection to the deeper truths of existence. It is always shining, always available. But if the windows of the lighthouse are dirty, covered in dust and grime from years of self-doubt, fear, and limiting beliefs, the light can't shine through as clearly.

Reclaiming your power is about **cleaning the windows**, wiping away the layers of conditioning, fear, and disempowerment that have clouded your view. When the windows are clean, your light shines brightly, effortlessly illuminating everything around you. **This is true empowerment.**

You don't need to seek power; you only need to allow it to flow through you. And when you align with that power, you stop living reactively—constantly responding to external circumstances—and begin living **creatively**, shaping your reality from the inside out.

Co-Creating with the Universe

This brings us to a crucial point: **You are a co-creator of your reality**. This is not just a metaphor—it's the mechanism of how the universe works. Your thoughts, emotions, and energy shape the reality you experience.

You are not a passive participant in life; you are actively co-creating it with every thought you think, every belief you hold, and every action you take.

Let's break this down: Everything in the universe is energy. Your thoughts, your feelings, your body—it's all energy vibrating at different frequencies. When you think a thought or hold a belief, you are emitting a frequency, like a radio transmitter. That frequency goes out into the universe, attracting experiences that match its vibration.

This is the essence of **manifestation**: you attract what you are aligned with. If you believe you are powerless, you will attract situations that reinforce that belief. If you believe you are capable, worthy, and empowered, you will attract opportunities that reflect that truth.

But here's the catch: **You can't fake alignment.** You can't just say, "I'm powerful" on the surface while still holding onto deep-seated beliefs of unworthiness or fear. The universe responds to your true vibration, not the words you say. This is why **inner work** is so important. To truly co-create with the universe, you must first clean the windows of your lighthouse—releasing limiting beliefs and realigning with your infinite power.

The Power of Intention, Thought, and Energy

Your thoughts are powerful, but **thoughts alone are not enough**. Many people misunderstand manifestation, thinking that if they just think positively, they will attract what they desire. But thoughts are only one part of the equation.

Intention is the driving force behind thought. It's the energy that powers your desires and gives them direction. When your thoughts are aligned with a clear intention, they become far more powerful. But even intention is not enough on its own.

To truly manifest your desires, you must align your **thoughts, emotions, and energy**. If your thoughts are saying one thing ("I want success") but your energy is vibrating with doubt or fear ("I'm afraid of failure"), your manifestation will be conflicted. The universe responds to your **energy**—the vibration of your entire being, not just your conscious thoughts.

Think of it like planting a seed. Your **thought** is the seed you plant, your **intention** is the soil, and your **energy** is the water and sunlight that allow it to grow. Without aligning all three, the seed won't take root.

This is why reclaiming your power means going deeper than just surface-level thinking. It's about aligning your entire being with the truth of who you are—your thoughts, your emotions, your energy all working in harmony to create the life you desire.

Living from a Place of True Power

So, how do you live from a place of **true power**? It starts with recognizing that power is not something you have to earn or acquire. It's something you already possess. **Empowerment is about aligning with that truth and living from it.**

When you live from a place of true power, you stop looking for validation from the outside world. You stop waiting for permission to be who you are. You stop measuring your worth by external standards—whether it's success, money, or approval. True power comes from within, and it is not dependent on anything outside of you. It is the quiet confidence that comes from knowing who you are, from being aligned with your highest self. It is the ability to stand in your truth, even when the world around you is trying to tell you otherwise.

Living from a place of true power means trusting yourself, trusting your intuition, and trusting the flow of life. It means recognizing that you are a co-creator of your reality and that you have the power to shape your life from the inside out.

Conclusion: Embodying Infinite Power

Empowerment is not about controlling the world around you—it's about **mastering the world within you**. It's about reclaiming the infinite power that is your birthright and using it to shape your reality with intention, clarity, and alignment.

You are more powerful than you've been taught to believe. The truth of who you are is limitless, expansive, and deeply connected to the flow of the universe. When you align with that truth, when you reclaim your power from the fear and limitations that have kept you small, you step into a new way of being—one where you are the conscious creator of your life, not a victim of circumstance.

This is your power: the ability to choose, to align, and to create from the infinite potential that exists within you. Reclaim it, embody it, and let it shape your life in ways that go beyond anything you've imagined.

Chapter 6: God — Redefining Divinity

The word "God" can provoke strong reactions—some filled with reverence, others with skepticism or even fear. For many, the concept of God has been handed down through rigid beliefs, traditions, or systems of thought. God is often portrayed as a figure outside of us, watching from a distance, perhaps even judging our every move. But is that really who or what God is?

This chapter invites you to explore the concept of **divinity** with fresh eyes, free from the limitations and dogmas that may have shaped your understanding. We are going to **redefine what God means**, moving beyond the old, limiting narratives of a distant deity to an expanded, more personal understanding of the divine essence that is not only all around you, but also within you. This is not about adopting new religious ideas or rejecting old ones; it's about expanding your understanding of God to match the depth and power of your true nature.

We are going to dive deep into this redefinition, challenging the idea of separation between you and the divine, and helping you realize that you are not just a creation of God—you are an expression of God.

What is God?

This is the central question that has puzzled humanity for millennia: *What is God?*

For centuries, many have believed in the idea of God as a **supreme being,** a father-like figure who rules over the universe, controlling fate and determining right from wrong. In this traditional view, God is separate from humanity—existing "out there" somewhere, in the heavens or beyond space and time. We are taught that we must seek God, that we must worship and serve God in order to be worthy of divine love or acceptance.

But let's challenge that narrative. Let's ask a question that goes to the very heart of this belief: *Why would an all-powerful, infinite being need anything from us?* Why would a God, whose essence is limitless, require worship, obedience, or devotion in order to love or accept us? Does that idea resonate with your deepest understanding of love and divinity?

Let's redefine what **God** could mean. Rather than viewing God as a being separate from us, what if we understand God as the **source of all that is**—the infinite creative force that is not only the origin of the universe but also the essence of every particle within it? What if God is not something or someone "out there," but the very fabric of existence itself—the energy that flows through everything, including you?

In this view, God is not a distant figure to be sought but a **presence to be experienced**—not a ruler or a judge, but the underlying **consciousness** that connects and unifies all of life. God is the spark of life in every living thing, the force that moves through the cosmos, and the light that exists within every human soul.

Moving Beyond Traditional Definitions

We live in a time where traditional definitions of God are being questioned, where people are seeking a more personal, expansive understanding of divinity. Many spiritual traditions, especially in the West, have portrayed God in human terms—a father figure, a king, or a judge. These portrayals were often designed to help people relate to the concept of God, but they also created limitations.

The idea of **anthropomorphizing** God—giving God human traits—can lead to a perception of separation. If God is a figure outside of us, above us, or watching over us, then it suggests a distance, a gap that we must bridge through prayer, devotion, or good behavior. But what if there is no distance? What if that separation is an illusion?

Let's explore a more expansive understanding: God as **consciousness itself**. Think of consciousness as the field in which all of existence takes place. It is not confined to a single being, location, or form. Consciousness is both **transcendent** (beyond all things) and **immanent** (within all things). This is the view that God is not a being in the sky but the essence of the sky, the earth, the universe—and most importantly, **the essence within you**.

Imagine the ocean. Every wave that rises and falls is an expression of the ocean's energy, yet no wave is separate from the ocean. You are the wave, and God is the ocean. You rise out of that infinite source, express yourself in this moment of life, and ultimately return to the same source. In this view, God is not a distant force, but the very essence of **who you are**—and you are an expression of that divine consciousness.

Oneness — The Divine Within All Things

This brings us to the idea of **oneness**. If God is the infinite source of all life, then everything that exists is part of God. There is no separation. You are not separate from the universe, from nature, from others, or from the divine. This understanding of oneness breaks down the false divisions that we've been taught to believe—divisions between people, between nations, between species, and between us and the divine.

Let's use another analogy. Imagine a vast web, stretching infinitely in all directions. Every strand of the web is connected to every other strand. A movement in one part of the web is felt throughout the entire structure. **This is the nature of oneness**—everything is interconnected, and nothing exists in isolation. God is not separate from this web; God *is* the web, the energy that connects all things. When you understand this, it changes how you view yourself and others. You are not a separate individual living in a disconnected world; you are part of a greater whole. **Divinity flows through you**, just as it flows through every living being. This understanding leads to profound compassion, empathy, and connection. You begin to see the divine spark in every person you meet, in every tree, in every star, and in every experience.

But this also means that the **divine is within you**. This is not a metaphor—it is a truth that becomes more apparent the deeper you connect with your own consciousness.

You are not just connected to the divine; **you are an expression of the divine**. God is not something you must search for outside of yourself—God is within you, as you, waiting to be realized and experienced.

Living as a Reflection of Divinity

If this is true—if you are a direct expression of divine consciousness—then the way you live your life becomes a reflection of that truth. To **live as a reflection of divinity** means to embody the qualities of the divine in your everyday life. These qualities are not distant ideals but inherent aspects of who you already are: love, compassion, creativity, wisdom, and unity.

But here's the challenge: most of us have forgotten our divine nature. We've been taught to believe that we are separate, that we are incomplete, that we must struggle to prove our worthiness. This belief in separation causes us to live in fear, doubt, and insecurity. It causes us to forget the truth of who we are.

To live as a reflection of divinity, you must first **remember who you are**. You are not a flawed, separate being struggling to find your place in the world. You are a spark of divine consciousness, capable of creating, loving, and experiencing life from a place of infinite potential.

This doesn't mean you will never face challenges or obstacles. But when you understand your divine nature, you approach those challenges from a place of empowerment, knowing that you are connected to an infinite source of wisdom, strength, and love. **You are not powerless; you are powerful beyond measure.** The divine within you is always available, always guiding you, always flowing through you—whether you are aware of it or not.

Think about the way you show up in the world. Are you living from a place of fear, trying to control outcomes, and seeking validation from external sources? Or are you living from a place of deep connection, trusting the flow of life, and embodying the divine qualities within you?

Experiencing God as a Living Presence

One of the most powerful shifts in understanding comes when you stop thinking about God as a concept and start experiencing God as a **living presence** in your life. This experience isn't reserved for a select few mystics or saints—it's available to you, right here, right now.

How do you experience this presence? By cultivating **awareness**. The divine presence is always here, but often we are too distracted, too caught up in the noise of daily life, to notice it. Experiencing God requires **stillness**, a willingness to quiet the mind and listen to the deeper currents of life flowing through you.

Meditation, mindfulness, and prayer are some of the ways you can open yourself to this experience. But it doesn't require formal practice. You can experience God in the simplicity of being present—whether it's watching a sunset, feeling the wind on your skin, or simply sitting in silence and allowing yourself to be. **The divine presence is always here, because it is who you are.** The more you practice becoming aware of this presence, the more it will become a natural part of your experience.

And here's an important point: **God is not separate from your everyday life**. The divine presence is just as available in your mundane tasks as it is in moments of deep reflection. Washing the dishes, talking to a friend, walking down the street—each of these moments is an opportunity to experience the divine. God is not found only in the extraordinary; **God is found in everything, including you.**

God and Co-Creation

Finally, let's explore the idea of **co-creation**. If you are an expression of divine consciousness, then you are also a **co-creator** with the divine. This means that your thoughts, intentions, and actions are not just passive responses to life—they are creative forces shaping the reality you experience. The universe is not static; it is in a constant state of becoming. And you, as an expression of divine consciousness, have the power to influence that becoming. Every thought you think, every emotion you feel, and every intention you set is a vibration that ripples out into the universe, creating and shaping your reality. This is not just a mystical idea—it's a fundamental truth of how energy works.

When you align yourself with the divine presence within you, you begin to **co-create** with the universe. You are no longer trying to force outcomes or control life from a place of fear or lack. Instead, you are flowing with the natural currents of creation, trusting in the intelligence and love of the divine source to guide you. **This is co-creation: the harmonious dance between you and the infinite, between your free will and the divine flow of life.**

Conclusion: Embracing Your Divine Nature

This chapter is not just about understanding God differently—it's about **experiencing God** in a way that transforms how you live. When you redefine divinity as the infinite presence within and around you, you begin to live from a place of deep connection, empowerment, and love. You stop searching for God in distant places and start recognizing the divine in every moment, in every being, and in yourself.

You are an expression of God. You are not separate from the divine; you are a part of it. And when you live from this truth, your life becomes an expression of divinity itself—filled with love, creativity, compassion, and purpose.

This is your divine nature: to live as an expression of the infinite, co-creating with the universe, and experiencing life in its fullness. You are not separate from God—you are a reflection of God's love, power, and presence in this world. Embrace that truth, and let it guide every step of your journey.

Chapter 7: Prayer and Manifestation — Conversations with the Infinite

Prayer is often seen as a one-way street—something you do when you need help, when you're lost, or when you're searching for meaning. It's a practice many associate with religion, perhaps an act of desperation or hope. But prayer, in its deepest sense, is far more than asking for something outside of yourself to intervene in your life.

True prayer is a **conversation with the infinite**, an intimate dialogue between you and the universe, between you and the divine essence that exists both within and around you. And when this conversation is aligned, something miraculous happens: **you become the bridge between the invisible and the visible**, between intention and reality. Prayer becomes the starting point of **manifestation**—the art of bringing the unseen into the seen, the formless into form.

This chapter invites you to reimagine both **prayer and manifestation** as dynamic, creative processes. It's not about pleading for help or luck. It's about aligning yourself with the flow of the universe, harnessing your divine power, and co-creating your reality from a place of deep connection with all that is.

The True Nature of Prayer

Many of us were taught that prayer is an act of asking—asking God, the universe, or some higher power to intervene, to solve our problems, or to bring us what we desire. And while there's nothing wrong with asking for guidance or help, this limited view of prayer places us in a position of separation. It reinforces the belief that we are down here, struggling, and God is somewhere far away, deciding whether or not to answer our calls.

But what if prayer is not about asking for intervention, but about **alignment**?

Let's redefine prayer as the act of **aligning your energy, thoughts, and intentions with the flow of the universe**. It's not a passive act of hope or desperation; it's an active, creative process. When you pray, you're not begging for help—you're entering into a **state of connection** with the divine energy that moves through all things, including you. You are aligning yourself with the frequency of the infinite, tuning your energy to the vibration of what you seek to create or experience.

Imagine a tuning fork. When you strike it, the fork vibrates at a specific frequency, and if you bring another tuning fork close to it, it will begin to vibrate at the same frequency. **Prayer is like striking that first tuning fork**. When you pray from a place of alignment, you vibrate at the frequency of the reality you wish to create, and the universe responds by matching that frequency, bringing your desires, intentions, or needs into form. It's not about asking for something to be handed to you—it's about becoming a vibrational match to the reality you wish to experience.

Prayer as a State of Being

Prayer is not just something you do in moments of need or reflection; **prayer is a state of being**. Every thought you think, every emotion you feel, and every intention you set is a form of prayer. Whether you're conscious of it or not, you are constantly sending out prayers— through your words, your thoughts, and your energy.

The question is: **What are you praying for?**

When you live in a state of fear, lack, or doubt, you are unintentionally praying for more of those experiences. Your energy is vibrating at the frequency of fear or scarcity, and the universe responds to that vibration by matching it. But when you shift your internal state—when you align yourself with love, abundance, and trust—you change the nature of your prayer. You begin to pray for and attract experiences that match the frequency of those higher states.

Here's an essential truth: **The universe doesn't respond to the words you say; it responds to the energy you embody.** You can pray with words all you want, but if your inner state is one of fear, lack, or desperation, that's the energy you are putting out into the world. On the other hand, if you enter a state of calm, trust, and connection, even without saying a word, that energy becomes your prayer. You are praying not with your words, but with your being.

Manifestation: Bringing the Unseen into Form

Now that we've redefined prayer, let's dive into **manifestation**. Manifestation is often misunderstood as a technique for getting what you want. People talk about "manifesting" success, love, wealth—treating it like a tool to manipulate the universe into delivering their desires. But this approach misses the true essence of manifestation.

At its core, manifestation is not about **getting** something; it's about **creating** alignment between the inner and outer worlds. It's about becoming a clear channel through which the invisible can become visible, the formless can take form. And this is where the relationship between prayer and manifestation becomes clear: **prayer is the process of aligning with the universe, and manifestation is the result of that alignment.**

Let's break this down into a mechanism:

1. **Intention**: The first step of manifestation is intention. This is where you set a clear, focused desire for what you wish to experience. But this intention must come from a place of **authenticity**. It's not enough to say, "I want this" without truly feeling aligned with it. The universe responds to genuine intention—one that is connected to your higher purpose, not just superficial desires.

2. **Alignment**: After setting your intention, you must align your thoughts, emotions, and energy with that intention. This is where prayer comes in, not as a request but as a practice of **becoming**

the vibration of what you wish to manifest. If you want to manifest love, for example, you must first **be** love—embody the energy of love in your thoughts, your emotions, and your interactions with the world. The same goes for abundance, success, peace, or any other desire.

3. **Trust and Surrender**: This is perhaps the most challenging part of manifestation—letting go. Once you have set your intention and aligned with it, you must **release your need to control the outcome**. This is where trust comes in. You trust that the universe knows the right time, the right way, and the right path for your desire to come into form. Surrender doesn't mean giving up on your desire—it means letting go of the need to force it, allowing the natural flow of the universe to bring it into being.

4. **Action**: Manifestation is not a passive process. Once you've aligned your energy and set your intention, you must take **inspired action**. This doesn't mean frantically trying to "make" things happen. It means listening to your intuition and taking steps that feel aligned with the energy of your intention. The universe will guide you

through signs, opportunities, and insights, but you must be willing to take action when the moment feels right.

The Role of Surrender and Trust in Manifestation

Many people struggle with manifestation because they cling too tightly to their desired outcome. They set an intention, but then they become obsessed with how it's going to happen, when it's going to happen, and whether or not they're doing it "right." This attachment to the outcome creates resistance, blocking the flow of energy between you and the universe.

Surrender is the key to unlocking the full power of manifestation. To surrender means to let go of your attachment to the "how" and the "when." It means trusting that the universe, in its infinite wisdom, will bring about your desire in the perfect way, even if that way doesn't match your expectations. This can be difficult, especially when we are conditioned to believe that control equals power. But true power lies in **trust**, not in control.

Think about a seed. When you plant a seed in the ground, you don't stand over it, demanding that it grow on your schedule. You water it, give it sunlight, and then you trust the natural process of growth. You know that the seed will grow in its own time, in its own way, without your interference. Manifestation works the same way. You plant the seed of intention, align your energy with that intention, and then you trust the universe to take care of the rest. **Surrender is not passive—it is an act of profound trust in the natural flow of life.**

Prayer and Manifestation as a Partnership

Now, let's bring it all together. **Prayer and manifestation are not separate practices—they are partners in the creative process.** Prayer is how you align with the universe, how you tune into the divine flow of life. Manifestation is the natural result of that alignment, the way the universe responds to your vibration.

When you engage in true prayer, you are not asking the universe for favors. You are aligning your inner world with the outer flow of creation. You are becoming a vibrational match for the reality you wish to experience. And when that alignment is strong, manifestation happens naturally. The universe responds to your vibration, bringing your desires into form with ease and grace.

A Shift in Perception: Becoming the Creator

Here's where the real shift happens: **You are not just a receiver of divine gifts—you are a creator.** The same divine force that created the stars, the oceans, and the universe flows through you. You have the power to shape your reality through the energy you embody, the intentions you set, and the alignment you cultivate.

This doesn't mean that you control everything that happens in your life. Life is a co-creative process, and there are forces beyond your control. But it does mean that you have the power to influence your experience of life. You can shape your reality by aligning with the energy of what you wish to create. This is the essence of **empowerment**—knowing that you are not a victim of circumstances, but a co-creator of your life.

When you engage in prayer and manifestation from this place of empowerment, you stop feeling like life is happening *to* you, and you start realizing that life is happening *through* you. You become an active participant in the unfolding of your own destiny, not by controlling outcomes, but by aligning with the flow of the universe and trusting in your own creative power.

Conclusion: Living Prayer, Living Manifestation

This chapter is about more than just redefining prayer and manifestation. It's about realizing that you are always in conversation with the universe, whether you're aware of it or not. **Every thought, every intention, every action is a prayer.** And every prayer is the starting point of manifestation.

Living prayer means being conscious of the energy you are putting into the world. It means recognizing that your inner state shapes your outer reality, and that alignment is the key to bringing your desires into form. Living manifestation means trusting the process, surrendering control, and taking inspired action when the time is right.

When you live in alignment with the divine flow, prayer and manifestation become natural extensions of who you are. **You are not separate from the divine—you are a co-creator with it**. The power to shape your reality is within you, waiting for you to recognize and embody it.

This is the invitation: to live in a state of conscious prayer, to co-create your reality with the infinite, and to trust in the natural flow of life as you bring your desires into being. The universe is always listening, always responding. **The question is, what are you praying** for—and are you ready to live the manifestation of that prayer?

Chapter 8: Cosmic Forms of Life — We Are Not Alone

We tend to think of life as something confined to Earth, limited to what we can observe, touch, and study. But let's challenge that perspective. For centuries, humans have looked up at the stars and wondered, *Are we truly alone? Is there life beyond what we know?* These questions aren't just about extraterrestrial beings or science fiction—they're about expanding our perception of what life really is and our connection to the **cosmos**.

This chapter is not simply about imagining little green men in UFOs. It's about recognizing that life, consciousness, and intelligence exist beyond the physical forms we are familiar with, and that they are part of the same vast, interconnected web of existence that we are. It's time to expand our understanding and realize that **we are not alone**—not in the way we experience life on Earth, nor in the larger, cosmic sense.

Expanding Our Awareness to Other Life Forms

When we talk about "life," we tend to limit the definition to what we know—biological organisms that breathe, reproduce, and exist within the confines of our atmosphere. But let's break free from that limited view. **Life, in its infinite forms, cannot be contained by our current understanding.**

The universe is vast beyond comprehension—there are trillions of galaxies, each containing billions of stars, many with planets that could potentially harbor life. And yet, despite the immensity of the cosmos, many of us hold onto the narrow belief that Earth is the only place where life exists. This is not only statistically improbable, but it also speaks to our limited perception of life itself.

Here's the first shift in thinking: **Life is not limited to physical, carbon-based organisms.** We know that on Earth, life takes many forms—from the smallest bacteria to the largest animals. But why would life in the cosmos need to conform to the same rules? Imagine consciousness and life in forms that are not based on the physical matter we know, but in energetic forms, in dimensions beyond the third, where beings exist not in flesh and blood, but as pure consciousness, light, or energy.

We already know, scientifically, that there are dimensions beyond our perception. If life is energy, if consciousness is the foundation of existence, then there are likely **cosmic life forms**—beings, intelligences, or consciousnesses that exist in these higher dimensions. They may not be visible to the human eye, but that doesn't mean they don't exist. Just as we can't see radio waves or ultraviolet light without the right tools, we may not yet have the full capacity to perceive the life forms that exist beyond our physical world.

Other forms of life in the universe may exist not just in faraway planets, but in dimensions that coexist with our own.

What Does It Mean to Be "Alive"?

This brings us to an important question: *What does it really mean to be alive?*

We are conditioned to believe that life must follow certain rules—there must be growth, reproduction, biological processes. But life is much more than biology. At its core, **life is consciousness**—the awareness of existence, the experience of being. If we define life as the presence of consciousness, then we must open ourselves to the possibility that life exists in many forms, far beyond what we've been taught to recognize.

Let's consider the possibility that the **universe itself is alive**. The galaxies, the stars, the planets—each a form of consciousness expressing itself through different means. There may be forms of life that are so vast, so interconnected, that they function on a cosmic scale. Just as a single cell in your body is part of a larger organism, individual planets or solar systems may be part of a larger, living network—a cosmic organism, if you will.

Think of this: on Earth, the cells in your body operate with their own intelligence. They live, they die, they multiply, and yet they are part of something much larger—you. Similarly, Earth may be one "cell" in the larger body of the universe, and just as your cells aren't aware of your thoughts or emotions, we may not be fully aware of the **cosmic intelligence** we are a part of.

Higher-Dimensional Beings and Parallel Realities

As we expand our understanding of life beyond Earth, we also need to broaden our perception of **what life can be** in higher dimensions and parallel realities. As we discussed earlier, dimensions beyond the third exist, and life forms in these dimensions are not bound by the same limitations of space, time, and matter that we are. These **higher-dimensional beings** may not have physical bodies as we know them, but that doesn't make them any less real. In fact, many spiritual traditions speak of **light beings**, **guides**, or **ascended masters**—entities that exist beyond the physical realm, in higher states of consciousness.

Just because we don't perceive these beings with our physical senses doesn't mean they don't interact with our world. In fact, there are countless accounts throughout history of people encountering these beings during moments of expanded consciousness—through meditation, near-death experiences, dreams, or spiritual practice. These beings may serve as guides or helpers, offering insights or protection to those who are open to their presence.

But why don't we see them more clearly? The answer lies in our **perception**. Just as radio waves exist all around us, yet we can't hear them unless we tune into the right frequency, these higher-dimensional beings exist in a frequency that most of us are not attuned to. As we develop our ability to tune into these higher frequencies—through expanded awareness, mindfulness, and inner alignment—we open ourselves to

direct communication and interaction with these beings.

The Role of Other Cosmic Life Forms in Humanity's Evolution

So, if there are other life forms in the cosmos—both physical and non-physical—what role do they play in our evolution as humans? Are they just distant observers, or is there a more active relationship between us and them?

Many spiritual traditions, as well as certain schools of thought in modern science, suggest that **humanity's evolution is not an isolated event**. We are part of a larger cosmic drama, a tapestry of life that spans the universe. Other life forms—whether physical beings from other planets or higher-dimensional entities—may play a crucial role in helping humanity evolve, not just technologically, but spiritually.

Let's consider the possibility that **cosmic life forms** have been guiding human evolution for millennia. There are countless ancient stories, myths, and legends from cultures around the world that speak of beings descending from the stars—gods, angels, or advanced civilizations that imparted knowledge to humanity. These stories may not be purely symbolic. What if these beings are real, and their role has been to help guide humanity's development? Just as a gardener nurtures a plant, ensuring it has the right conditions to grow, these beings may be assisting humanity in its evolution, helping us expand our consciousness, overcome our limitations, and evolve beyond the narrow confines of our current understanding.

But it's important to recognize that these beings do not control us or dictate our future. **Humanity's evolution is a co-creative process.** We are not passive participants in this cosmic dance. We have free will, and we are active co-creators in our own development. These beings may offer guidance, but it is up to us to choose how we grow, how we evolve, and how we expand our awareness.

Connecting and Coexisting with Cosmic Life

So, how do we connect with these cosmic life forms— beings of light, higher-dimensional guides, or even potential extraterrestrial civilizations? The answer lies in expanding our perception and **raising our vibration** to meet them halfway.

Cosmic beings are not distant or inaccessible. They are part of the same universal energy that flows through all things. The key to connecting with them is not through technology or space travel, but through inner alignment, meditation, and conscious awareness. When you raise your vibration—through practices like meditation, mindfulness, and living in alignment with your highest self—you begin to **tune into the frequency** where these beings exist.

This is not a mystical or magical process. It's a natural result of expanding your consciousness. Just as you can tune a radio to pick up different stations, you can tune your consciousness to perceive higher-dimensional beings and energies. **Cosmic life forms are always present**, always interacting with our world, but most of us are not aware of it because we're tuned into the frequency of the physical world. When you expand your awareness beyond the physical, you open yourself to these cosmic connections.

Coexisting with cosmic life means recognizing that **we are part of a larger, interconnected whole**. The universe is teeming with life—physical, energetic, and beyond. The more we open ourselves to this truth, the more we realize that we are not separate from the cosmos, but deeply connected to it.

What Cosmic Life Means for Humanity's Future

The recognition that we are not alone in the universe has profound implications for humanity's future. It challenges us to rethink our place in the cosmos, to expand our understanding of what it means to be alive, and to reconsider how we treat each other and the planet we inhabit.

Imagine the impact it would have on human consciousness if we fully accepted that we are part of a **cosmic community**. It would dissolve the false barriers that divide us—national borders, racial differences, and the illusion of separateness. We would begin to see ourselves not as isolated beings struggling to survive in a hostile universe, but as part of a larger, cosmic family, working together for the evolution and upliftment of all life.

When humanity fully embraces its connection to other forms of life in the universe, it will mark the beginning of a new era—an era of **expanded consciousness**, where we understand our place in the cosmos, not as solitary beings, but as interconnected participants in the grand dance of existence.

This shift in perspective will also change how we approach life on Earth. We will begin to see the planet itself as a living, conscious being—part of the larger cosmic ecosystem. The way we treat Earth, each other, and the universe will shift from one of exploitation and division to one of respect, harmony, and unity.

Conclusion: Expanding into the Cosmic Consciousness

The universe is vast, and the possibilities for life are endless. To believe that we are the only conscious beings in this infinite expanse is not only limiting but also diminishes our potential for growth and connection. **We are not alone**, and as we expand our awareness, we begin to realize that the cosmos is alive with consciousness—life in forms both familiar and beyond our imagination.

This chapter is an invitation to expand your perception of life beyond Earth, beyond the physical, and into the **cosmic reality** that surrounds us. The universe is teeming with intelligence, consciousness, and life in ways that we are only beginning to understand. As we open ourselves to this truth, we begin to see that we are part of something far greater than we ever imagined. **We are not alone**, and as we recognize our connection to cosmic life, we also recognize our role in the ongoing evolution of consciousness—on Earth and beyond. The universe is waiting for us to awaken to this truth, to step into our place in the cosmic family, and to live in alignment with the greater whole.

The question is: **Are we ready to embrace the vastness of who we truly are?**

Chapter 9: Living Fully Connected — Merging Spirit with the Physical

We live in a world that often feels divided. There's the physical world—the tangible reality we wake up to every day: the bills, the responsibilities, the to-do lists. Then, there's the spiritual world—the realm of intuition, inner guidance, and connection to something greater than ourselves. For most people, these two realities feel separate, almost in conflict. We are taught to believe that success in the material world requires sacrificing our spiritual growth, and that living a spiritual life means abandoning the physical.

But this division is an illusion. **You are both spirit and body**, both eternal consciousness and a physical being. The true challenge and the ultimate goal of this life is to bring those two aspects into harmony—to **live fully connected**, integrating the infinite power of your spiritual nature with the everyday experiences of the physical world. This is not just about finding balance; it's about **merging** the two, so that your spirit is expressed through every action, thought, and experience in this life.

This chapter is an invitation to embody your infinite potential while fully engaging with the physical world.

You'll learn how to bring spiritual awareness into every aspect of your life, to live with purpose and passion, and to fully trust in the unfolding of your journey.

What Does It Mean to Live Fully Connected?

To **live fully connected** means to recognize and embrace the truth that you are an infinite being having a physical experience. It means understanding that your physical life—your body, your work, your relationships—are not separate from your spiritual path. They are the **expression** of your spirit in this world.

Imagine living every moment of your life with the awareness that the divine is flowing through you, that your every action is a reflection of your highest self. You are not waiting for some future moment to "arrive" at a spiritual understanding or enlightenment. You are living it now, in every breath, in every conversation, in every challenge.

Living fully connected doesn't mean retreating from the world to meditate on a mountain or disengaging from the physical. It means embracing the material world as a canvas for your spiritual expression. **Your physical life is not an obstacle to spiritual growth; it is the platform for it.** Every interaction, every decision, every experience is an opportunity to express your highest nature—to bring the infinite into the finite, the formless into form.

The Formula: Aligning with Your Highest Passion

To live fully connected, you must first learn to **align with your highest passion or excitement**. This is the doorway to your highest self. Think of passion or excitement as a direct line to your soul, your inner compass pointing you toward the actions, experiences, and choices that are most aligned with who you truly are. When you follow that feeling of excitement, you are aligning with the **flow of the universe**—moving in harmony with the life that wants to unfold through you.

The formula is simple yet powerful:

1. **Act on your highest passion or excitement to the best of your ability, in every moment.**

2. **Keep a positive state of being, trusting that whatever life brings you is for your highest purpose.**

3. **Have zero expectations about what the outcome should be.**

Let's break this formula down and explore its power.

Step 1: Act on Your Highest Passion or Excitement

This is the starting point: **Act on your highest passion, your highest excitement, in every moment, to the best of your ability.** This doesn't mean only pursuing your "dream job" or waiting for the perfect opportunity. It means following the **thread of excitement** in whatever form it shows up in your life, right now. Maybe you're at work and a sudden idea excites you—act on that. Maybe you feel a spark of joy when thinking about calling a friend or starting a creative project—follow that. **Passion is the language of your soul**, guiding you toward the actions that are most aligned with your highest potential.

Passion is not something that only exists in grand moments or major life changes. It's available to you in every small action, every choice, every decision. When you act on your highest passion in the present moment, no matter how small it seems, you are aligning with the flow of the universe. You are following the **path of least resistance**—the path where energy flows most freely.

Think of your passion as a river. When you act on it, you allow the current of the river to carry you forward. When you ignore it, you are swimming upstream, fighting against the natural flow of life. **Your highest excitement is the current that leads you effortlessly toward your highest potential.**

Step 2: Keep a Positive State of Being

Once you are acting on your highest passion, the next crucial step is to maintain a **positive state of being**. This means that, regardless of the external circumstances, you hold a deep, inner knowing that everything happening in your life is unfolding for your highest purpose.

This step requires **trust**—trust that life is not random, that the challenges and obstacles you face are not roadblocks, but stepping stones. Even when things don't go as planned, when the path is unclear, or when you face difficulties, **trust that the universe is working in your favor**. Every experience is an opportunity for growth, expansion, and deeper alignment with your true self.

This positive state of being is not about ignoring difficult emotions or pretending everything is perfect. It's about embracing the **wholeness** of your experience—understanding that both the highs and the lows are part of your growth. When you trust the process, you stop resisting life. You stop trying to control every outcome, and instead, you allow life to guide you, knowing that **everything serves your highest evolution**.

Think of a tree in a storm. The wind may bend its branches, but the tree doesn't fight the wind. It bends and sways, trusting that the storm will pass, and it will grow stronger because of it. **Your life is like that tree**. The storms will come, but if you trust in the process, you will grow stronger, more resilient, and more connected to your true self.

Step 3: Have Zero Expectations

This is perhaps the most challenging part of the formula, but it's also the most liberating: **Have zero expectations about what the outcome ought to be.** Why is this so important? Expectations create **resistance**. When you act on your passion with the expectation of a specific result, you are narrowing the field of possibilities. You are essentially saying, "This is the only outcome that will make me happy or fulfilled." But the universe may have something far greater in store for you—something you can't yet see.

Having expectations is like planting a seed and then constantly digging it up to see if it's growing. You're interrupting the natural process. **When you have zero**

expectations, you allow life to unfold in its own way, in its own time. You free yourself from the burden of needing things to happen a certain way, and instead, you open yourself to the infinite possibilities that exist.

Here's the truth: **The universe always has a bigger plan than you can imagine.** When you let go of expectations, you give the universe the freedom to surprise you, to bring you something even better than what you thought you wanted. Expectations limit the potential of your experience because they come from the mind, which is conditioned to think in terms of past experiences and known possibilities. But **the universe operates on infinite possibilities**—it is not bound by what you think is possible.

By releasing expectations, you move into a state of **allowance**—you allow the universe to work through you, trusting that whatever comes is exactly what you need for your highest growth and expansion.

The Mechanics of the Formula: Trusting the Flow of Life

Let's explore the mechanics of how this formula works in real life.

Imagine you are standing at the edge of a river, holding a small boat. Your **highest passion** is the current of the river. When you place your boat in the water and let the current guide you, you are acting on that passion. But if you try to steer the boat in a specific direction, fighting against the current, you create resistance. The current will still take you where you need to go, but the journey becomes harder, slower, and more exhausting.

Now imagine you let go of the need to control the boat. You trust the current, knowing that it will carry you exactly where you need to be. You don't worry about the rocks or rapids ahead—you trust that the river knows the way. This is what it means to **act on your passion, stay in a positive state, and release expectations**. When you trust the flow of life, you allow the universe to guide you effortlessly toward your highest potential.

Here's the magic of this formula: **When you release expectations, you stop blocking the flow of abundance.** You open yourself to outcomes that are far greater than what you could have imagined. You allow the universe to deliver not just what you think you want, but what you truly need for your growth, joy, and expansion.

Why Zero Expectations Are Crucial for Living Fully Connected

The reason it's so important to have zero expectations is because **expectations come from the ego**. The ego is always trying to control, to predict, to manage outcomes. It fears the unknown and wants to feel secure by knowing what will happen next. But the truth is, the unknown is where **infinite possibilities** live. When you release the need to know or control the outcome, you open yourself to the magic of life.

Expectations are rooted in fear—fear that if things don't go a certain way, you'll be disappointed, or you won't be happy. But true empowerment comes from realizing that **joy, fulfillment, and growth are not tied to specific outcomes**. They are available to you in every moment, no matter what happens. When you stop attaching your happiness to specific results, you become free. You can flow with life, trusting that each moment is perfect, even if it doesn't look the way you expected.

Here's the paradox: When you have no expectations, you become more open to receiving everything you desire, and more. **Zero expectations don't limit you; they liberate you.** They allow you to receive from the universe in ways that are beyond your imagination, in ways that truly serve your highest purpose.

Living Fully Connected: Embodying the Formula

Living fully connected means embracing this formula as a way of being. It's about **showing up fully in each moment**, acting on your highest excitement, and trusting that life is unfolding perfectly, even when you don't understand how. It's about knowing that you are always guided, always supported, and always connected to the infinite flow of the universe.

This way of living is not about achieving perfection. It's about being **present** in the process—being fully engaged in your life, not from a place of fear or control, but from a place of trust and joy. When you live fully connected, you stop waiting for life to deliver happiness, and you start realizing that **happiness is available to you right now**, in this very moment, regardless of external circumstances.

Living fully connected means embracing your dual nature: You are both spirit and body, both infinite and physical. You are here to experience the fullness of life, to express your highest potential, and to co-create with the universe in every moment. And when you align with your highest passion, stay in a positive state, and release expectations, you begin to live from the infinite power that is your birthright.

Conclusion: The Freedom of Living Fully Connected

This chapter is about embracing the **freedom** that comes from living fully connected—from knowing that you are always aligned with the flow of life, even when things don't go as planned. It's about trusting that everything, every experience, is part of your highest purpose, and that the universe is always conspiring in **your favor.**

When you live fully connected, you stop trying to control life and start **dancing** with it. You become a co-creator, working in harmony with the universe, knowing that the path of your highest passion will always lead you to the experiences that serve your greatest growth and joy.

The formula—acting on your passion, staying positive, and releasing expectations—is not just a method for manifesting what you desire. It's a way of **being**, a way of living from your highest truth. It's about realizing that the true power of creation lies not in controlling the outcome, but in trusting the process, in flowing with the infinite intelligence that moves through all things.

When you live this way, you discover that life is not something happening *to* you—it is something happening *through* you. **You are the creator, the creation, and the flow itself.** And the more you trust this, the more fully you live, not just as a spiritual being or a physical being, but as a fully connected, infinite expression of life itself.

Conclusion: A Shift Begins with You — Awakening to the Truth of Your Existence

As we reach the conclusion of this first masterpiece, *Perception: Tome 1*, take a moment to pause and reflect on the journey we've been on together. This book, in its essence, is not just words on a page. It is a **call to awakening**, a gentle but profound invitation to see life in a way you may never have seen it before. Through the chapters, we've explored the very foundation of existence—time, death, purpose, dimensions, empowerment, the nature of God, the power of prayer and manifestation, and our connection to the cosmos. But this is not just a collection of abstract ideas; it is a roadmap for personal transformation.

This is where the shift begins: with you.

The Power of Perception: The Lens Through Which You Experience Life

Everything in life is shaped by the lens through which we perceive it. What you see, what you believe, and how you interpret your experiences are the building blocks of your reality. This entire book has been about **reclaiming**

that power—the power to reshape your lens of perception and, by doing so, reshape your experience of reality itself.

We began by exploring the illusion of **time**, realizing that we are not bound by linear pasts or anxious futures. Instead, we live in the **eternal Now**, where all potential exists. We then moved through the doorway of **death**, understanding that it is not an end but a transformation, a return to the infinite consciousness from which we came. And then we dove deep into **purpose**, unlocking the truth that purpose is not something to chase but something to embody, moment by moment, as we align with our true nature.

With each chapter, the illusion of separation began to dissolve—between you and time, between you and the divine, between you and the universe itself. We uncovered the **multidimensional reality** we live in, where life extends far beyond the limits of our five senses and physical bodies. We explored the nature of **empowerment**, realizing that true power is not about controlling life, but about aligning with it, co-creating with the universe through a deep, authentic connection to your inner self.

We saw that **God** is not an external figure, a distant deity sitting in judgment, but the very essence of life flowing through you. The divine is not separate from you—it is within you, as you. Prayer became redefined as a **conversation with the infinite**, not a request for favors but an alignment with the energy of creation itself. And manifestation was revealed as the natural result of living in that alignment, trusting the process, and releasing all expectations.

Finally, we expanded our view of **cosmic life**, realizing that we are not alone in the universe. Consciousness, life, and intelligence exist on levels far beyond what we have been taught to see, and these cosmic forms of life are part of the same interconnected web of existence that we are.

All of these truths bring us back to one central idea: **Perception shapes everything.**

A Shift Begins Within: Personal Transformation as the Catalyst for a New Reality

If there is one message that echoes through every page of this book, it is this: **The shift begins within.**

Every transformation, every new possibility, every expansion of consciousness begins with a personal awakening. You cannot change the world without first changing the way you see it. The world you experience is a reflection of your own inner state, your beliefs, your perceptions. If you want to see a different reality, if you want to experience life on a higher, more expanded level, then the shift must start from within.

This is the purpose of this book. It is a **manual for personal awakening**, an invitation to experience reality in a new way. Not through the limited lens of fear, lack, and separation, but through the lens of **infinite potential, unity, and empowerment**. This shift is not something you wait for—it's something you choose, moment by moment, as you peel away the layers of conditioning, false beliefs, and limiting perceptions that have kept you small.

You are the creator of your reality, and by shifting your perception, you begin to create a new experience of life. This is why personal transformation is not just important—it is essential. **Your life is the canvas upon which you paint the reality you wish to see.**

Living Fully Connected: Bringing the Infinite into the Physical

As we discussed in Chapter 9, living fully connected is about merging your **infinite, spiritual nature** with your physical experience. This is where the true shift happens—not by escaping the physical world, but by bringing your spiritual awareness into every aspect of your daily life.

This is not a spiritual journey that asks you to transcend or reject the material world. On the contrary, it asks you to fully **embrace** the material world as the platform for your spiritual expression. Every action you take, every decision you make, every interaction you have is an opportunity to express your divine nature. **This is how the shift happens—through you, in every moment.**

When you live fully connected, you stop seeing the physical world as something separate from your spiritual self. You stop waiting for some future moment to "arrive" at your purpose or enlightenment. You realize that **this is it**—this moment, this experience, this life is where your divine power is meant to be expressed.

This is how you begin to live a new reality—by aligning with your highest passion, trusting in the flow of life, and releasing the need to control outcomes. When you live in this way, the shift is not something that happens outside of you. **The shift happens through you.**

The Importance of a Collective Shift: Laying the Foundation for Perception Tome 2

While this book focuses on the **personal shift**, it is important to recognize that the transformation of society begins with the transformation of individuals. **Personal shifts create ripple effects**, and as more people begin to awaken to the truth of who they are, those ripples become waves, creating a broader societal shift.

The world we live in today is a reflection of the collective consciousness—the beliefs, fears, and perceptions held by the majority of people. If we want to see a world that is more just, more compassionate, more united, then the collective consciousness must evolve. **And that evolution begins with individuals.**

This is where the work of *Perception* continues. In **Tome 2**, we will explore the **societal shift** that is not only possible but necessary for humanity to thrive on a global scale. We will examine how the beliefs and structures that govern our societies—political systems, economies, social norms—are built on old paradigms of fear, control, and separation. And we will look at how these systems must evolve if we are to create a world that reflects the higher truths of unity, love, and empowerment that we've explored in this book.

But the foundation for that societal shift lies in the personal transformation we have explored in *Tome 1*. You cannot create a new society with the same level of consciousness that created the old one. **A shift in perception must happen first on the personal level**, and only then can it expand into a broader, societal transformation.

The personal and the collective are deeply intertwined. As you awaken, you naturally contribute to the awakening of others. As you shift your perception, you help create the fertile ground for a new way of being in the world—one based on love, unity, and collaboration, rather than fear, division, and control.

A New Reality is Waiting: The Shift is Now

So here we are, at the culmination of our journey. But in many ways, this is just the beginning. This book is an invitation to experience life on a different level, to open your mind and heart to new possibilities, and to step into the fullness of who you really are.

A new reality is waiting. It is not something in the distant future, or something that will arrive only when the world outside changes. It is available to you right now, in this moment. The shift begins within you, and as you change, so does your experience of life.

You don't need to wait for the world to change. You don't need to wait for permission or for the "right time." The shift is already happening. **You are the shift.**

By reclaiming your power, by realigning your perception, by living fully connected, you begin to experience reality on a higher level—a level where you are no longer bound by fear, limitation, or separation, but where you live as a conscious creator of your own experience, in harmony with the infinite intelligence of the universe.

This is the shift we have been waiting for. And it begins with you.

Looking Ahead: Perception Tome 2 — A Shift in Society

As we move forward from this personal transformation, the next phase of the journey takes us into the **societal shift**. *Perception: Tome 2* will explore how the broader structures of our world must evolve to reflect the higher consciousness that we are now stepping into. We will look at how political systems, economies, education, and social norms can transform to support a world where **unity, compassion, and empowerment** are the guiding principles.

But for now, the work is within. The work is to shift your own perception, to live from the truth of who you are, and to express that truth in every aspect of your life.

Thank you for joining me on this journey. Thank you for being open, for questioning, for exploring the depths of your own potential. The shift has already begun, and you are a crucial part of it.

Together, we are creating a new reality.

With all my love and gratitude for this journey we've walked together, **I thank you** for stepping into the fullness of who you are.

Vocabulary Explication: *Perception: Tome 1*

1. Alignment

Alignment is the state where your actions, thoughts, and feelings are in harmony with your highest self and the flow of the universe. It allows you to move effortlessly through life, guided by your inner truth rather than external pressures.

2. Awakening

Awakening refers to the process of becoming aware of deeper truths about your existence and your connection to the universe. It's the shift from seeing yourself as just a physical being to recognizing your infinite nature and the vast potential that exists within you.

3. Belief Systems

Belief systems are the mental frameworks that shape how we interpret and interact with the world. They can either limit or expand our experience of life, depending on whether they are based in fear and separation or in empowerment and unity.

4. Conscious Creation

Conscious creation is the process of intentionally shaping your reality by aligning your inner state with your external desires. It's about being a co-creator with the universe, manifesting your highest vision by acting from a place of awareness.

5. Consciousness

Consciousness is the awareness of existence, not just on an individual level, but as a universal force that underlies all things. In this book, consciousness is viewed as the essence of life, present in every aspect of reality, connecting everything.

6. Cosmic Intelligence

Cosmic intelligence is the organizing force behind the universe, often referred to as the source or divine consciousness. It governs everything from the movement of galaxies to the growth of a single flower. By tuning into this intelligence, we align ourselves with a greater purpose.

7. Dimensions

Dimensions refer to different levels of reality or consciousness beyond the physical three-dimensional world we experience with our senses. Higher dimensions are realms of greater awareness, where time, space, and energy operate differently, and where expanded forms of life and consciousness exist.

8. Duality

Duality is the perception of life as being divided into opposing forces, such as good and bad, light and dark, or body and spirit. Moving beyond duality means embracing the unity of all things and seeing contrasts as interconnected parts of a larger whole.

9. Ego

The ego is the aspect of the self that identifies with separateness, fear, and control. It seeks to define itself through external validation and material achievements but can limit your awareness of your true, infinite nature.

10. Energy

In *Perception: Tome 1*, energy refers to the vital life force that flows through all things. Everything in the universe, including thoughts and emotions, is made of energy vibrating at different frequencies. Shifting your energy can change your experiences and interactions with life.

11. Frequency

Frequency refers to the vibration of energy that determines the quality of your experiences. Higher frequencies are associated with states of love, joy, and peace, while lower frequencies correspond to fear, anger, and anxiety. By raising your frequency, you align with more positive and expansive states of being.

12. Higher Self

The higher self is the eternal, infinite aspect of your being that exists beyond the ego and physical limitations. It's the source of wisdom, intuition, and guidance that leads you toward your highest potential and purpose.

13. Manifestation

Manifestation is the process of bringing your inner desires into physical reality. It happens when your thoughts, emotions, and actions are in alignment with your intentions, allowing you to co-create your experiences with the universe.

14. Multidimensionality

Multidimensionality refers to the concept that existence operates on multiple levels or dimensions, some of which are beyond our physical perception. Life and consciousness can exist in various forms and frequencies, often unseen by our limited senses but connected to our reality.

15. Oneness

Oneness is the understanding that everything in existence is interconnected and comes from the same source. The illusion of separation is dissolved when we realize that we are part of a larger, unified whole, where every thought, action, and being is connected.

16. Perception

Perception is the lens through which you experience reality. It shapes how you interpret your life and the world around you. By shifting your perception, you can transform your reality, breaking free from limiting beliefs and embracing the infinite potential available to you.

17. Prayer

In *Perception: Tome 1*, prayer is redefined as a conversation with the infinite. It's less about asking for something and more about aligning your energy with the divine flow of creation, inviting you to co-create with the universe through conscious intention.

18. Quantum Field

The quantum field is the energetic realm where all possibilities exist simultaneously. It's a field of infinite potential, where thoughts, intentions, and emotions interact with energy to manifest realities. By tuning into this field, you can influence the outcomes of your life.

19. Shift

A shift refers to a profound change in awareness, perception, or consciousness. In the context of this book, the shift is the awakening process that allows you to break free from limiting beliefs and step into your full potential as an infinite being.

20. Spirit

Spirit refers to the non-physical essence of who you are, beyond the body and mind. It is your eternal, conscious self that is deeply connected to the divine, always present and guiding you toward growth and evolution.

21. Time (Illusion of Time)

In *Perception: Tome 1*, time is presented as an illusion. While we experience time in a linear way—past, present, future—true reality exists in the eternal Now, where all potential and possibilities reside. Understanding the illusion of time allows you to live more fully in the present moment.

22. Trust (Surrender)

Trust is the practice of releasing control and surrendering to the flow of life. It involves having faith in the universe's wisdom and timing, knowing that everything unfolds for your highest good, even if the outcomes are not what you initially expect.

23. Vibration

Vibration refers to the energetic quality of your being. Everything vibrates at a certain frequency, and your vibration determines the experiences, people, and circumstances you attract into your life. Raising your vibration is key to aligning with higher possibilities and living a more fulfilling life.

Sneak Peek: Perception Tome 2 — A Shift in Society

As we stand on the precipice of a new world, it becomes increasingly clear that the personal shift we've been cultivating must extend into the collective. The next great leap in human evolution is not simply one of individual awakening but of a societal transformation—a shift in how we live, how we govern, how we interact with one another, and how we align with the planet itself.

Perception: Tome 2 will explore how we take the principles of personal empowerment, spiritual connection, and alignment with the infinite and apply them to the structures that shape our world. This is not about tearing down systems out of anger or fear; it is about building new structures from a place of love, unity, and a deep understanding of our shared existence.

1. Redefining Leadership: Moving from Control to Collaboration

One of the first areas that must evolve is our concept of leadership. For centuries, leadership has been associated with control, power, and authority—often enforced through fear and division. In the new paradigm, leadership becomes a role of guidance, collaboration, and service. We will explore how future leaders can operate from a space of consciousness, leading not from ego but from a deep alignment with the collective good.

What does leadership look like when it is based on love rather than control? We'll explore examples of emerging leaders who are already embodying this shift and what we can do to cultivate these qualities in ourselves and our communities.

2. Economics of Abundance: Rewriting the Rules of Value

The current economic systems are built on the idea of scarcity—there's not enough, and you must compete for resources. This belief is reflected in everything from global markets to local economies, perpetuating inequality and lack. But what if the foundation of economics was abundance?

In **Tome 2**, we will dive deep into the concept of **economics based on abundance**—systems where resources are shared, value is not confined to money, and cooperation replaces competition. We'll explore new models of exchange that are emerging worldwide, from gifting economies to regenerative enterprises, and how they reflect our shift in consciousness.

What if wealth was measured not just in material assets but in well-being, creativity, and collective empowerment?

3. Education for Consciousness: Empowering Future Generations

Our current education system teaches us what to think, not how to think. It conditions young minds for conformity, not creativity. In a society aligned with higher consciousness, education must be fundamentally reimagined.

In the future, education will focus on nurturing each individual's unique gifts, encouraging exploration, curiosity, and inner wisdom. Instead of feeding children information to memorize, we will create environments that foster spiritual growth, emotional intelligence, and multidimensional thinking.

How do we educate the next generation to be leaders, creators, and conscious beings? We will explore the pioneering schools and methodologies that are already planting the seeds of this shift and how we can bring these ideas into our own lives and communities.

4. Healing the Planet: Living in Harmony with Earth

At the core of societal transformation is our relationship with the Earth. As we awaken to our deeper connection with all life, it becomes impossible to continue living in ways that harm the planet. Our current relationship with nature is one of exploitation and dominance, but the future demands a return to harmony, where humans act as stewards of the Earth rather than conquerors.

In **Tome 2**, we will explore the rise of sustainable living, permaculture, and regenerative practices that honor the Earth as a living being. We will also look at indigenous knowledge systems that have long understood the interconnectedness of all life, learning how to integrate these ancient wisdoms with modern technologies to create a world where humans and nature thrive together.

What does it mean to truly live in harmony with the Earth?

5. The Evolution of Relationships: From Transaction to Sacred Union

Our relationships—whether romantic, familial, or communal—are reflections of our inner state. In the old paradigm, relationships are often transactional: based on what we can give or get from one another. In the new world, relationships are seen as sacred unions—opportunities for growth, reflection, and the expression of divine love.

Tome 2 will explore the evolution of relationships, where the focus shifts from control, codependency, and attachment to co-creation, freedom, and deep connection. We will look at how conscious relationships transform not only our personal lives but also the collective, helping to anchor a new way of being in the world.

What does love look like when it is free of fear, judgment, and expectation?

6. A Global Awakening: The Birth of a New Civilization

The transformation we seek is not just personal or local—it is global. As more individuals awaken to their true nature, a new civilization begins to emerge, one where unity and diversity coexist, where borders no longer divide, and where peace is not an abstract concept but a lived reality.

Tome 2 will examine the global movements that are leading the way toward this new civilization. We'll explore examples of global collaboration, peace-building efforts, and technologies that bridge gaps rather than create them. As we awaken collectively, we move from a world of separation and competition to one of unity and cooperation.